GROWING
YOUR
OWN
BUSINESS

GROWING YOUR OWN

BUSINESS

GREGORY KISHEL
AND
PATRICIA KISHEL

A PERIGEE BOOK

A Perigee Book
Published by The Berkley Publishing Group
200 Madison Avenue
New York, NY 10016

Copyright © 1994 by Gregory Kishel and Patricia Kishel

Book design by Stanley S. Drate/Folio Graphics Co. Inc.

Cover design by David Bamford

First edition: October 1994

Published simultaneously in Canada.

Library of Congress Cataloging-in-Publication Data

Kishel, Gregory F., 1946–
    Growing your own business / by Gregory Kishel and Patricia Kishel.
    —1st Perigee ed.
        p.   cm.
    ISBN 0-399-52136-4
        1. New business enterprises.   2. Small business—Management.
    3. Entrepreneurship.   I. Kishel, Patricia Gunter, 1948–
    II. Title.
    HD62.5.K554   1994
    658.02′2—dc20   94-14006
                                                                    CIP

Printed in the United States of America

10   9   8   7   6   5   4   3   2   1

CONTENTS

PREFACE

Starting a business is one thing, making it succeed is another. Once the seed for a business has been planted, how do you make it grow? Picking up where other small-business management books leave off, *Growing Your Own Business* is designed to help you deal with the ongoing challenges you face once your business is up and running.

Going beyond the basics of how to start a business, each chapter addresses a *key decision area* of concern to business owners as their businesses grow (planning, expansion, control, personal involvement, taxes, transition, and more). Weighing both financial and personal concerns, the book provides you with the help you need at the point you need it the most—when the business decisions are more complex and the stakes are higher.

Step by step, decision by decision, *Growing Your Own Business* examines the pros and cons of various growth strategies, helping you to evaluate your options and choose the best course of action. You'll find the information you need to answer a host of "make or break" questions, including:

▶ How big should my business grow?
▶ Should I add or drop products?
▶ Enter a new field?
▶ Focus on a different target market?
▶ Change the image of the business?
▶ Hold a public stock offering?
▶ Sell franchises?
▶ Merge with another business?
▶ Be more or less involved in operations?
▶ Keep the business in the family or sell it?

Exploring these questions and more, this hands-on guide shows how you can avoid the pitfalls associated with growing a business and maximize your success. Whether your business is in manufacturing, retailing, or services, is just taking root or is already well established, you'll be better equipped to keep it on track and ahead of the pack.

1 | PREPARING A GROWTH PLAN

The single most important thing you can do to grow your business is to take the time to plan. The more effort you put into planning, the stronger your business will be. Obvious as that may seem, it's a step that entrepreneurs often want to avoid or delegate to someone else. In the rush to capitalize on a new trend, capture the market, or beat the competition, many business owners can't be bothered with planning. Instead, they charge blindly ahead without giving any thought to where they are going . . . or if it's even a place they want to be. "Action" becomes the watchword, short-term profits the goal instead of long-term progress.

It's true that entrepreneurs need to be able to move quickly and decisively to take advantage of opportunities. But, at the same time, you must think about the outcome of each move. Will pursuing one opportunity mean forgoing another? Do you have the necessary resources to succeed? Are the rewards worth the risk? Will it strengthen the business? Does it lead to something else you want to do? The only way to know the answers to these questions is by planning.

The need for a business plan becomes even more evident as your business grows and more people are involved in carrying out its activities. Information that once could have been known by you alone must be shared with others—managers, lenders, investors, and so on. The most efficient means for bringing everyone together toward a common objective is your business plan. Defining the goals of the business and its method for achieving them, the plan can serve as a blueprint for growing your business that everyone can follow.

LAYING THE FOUNDATION

In preparing a business plan you are laying the foundation for future growth, showing your business as it is and as you want it to be in years to come. While describing the nature of your business, its target market, resources and capabilities, strategies, competitive position, environment, and more, the plan can also help clarify the following:

▶ The purpose of your business
▶ Its strengths and weaknesses
▶ Which customers it should serve
▶ Who your competition is
▶ What changes are occurring in the marketplace
▶ What new opportunities are emerging
▶ What threats must be avoided
▶ What additional people are needed to meet your goals
▶ How much capital must be raised
▶ Ways to improve your product or service
▶ Ways to increase sales
▶ Which types of expansion methods to use
▶ How to cut costs and increase profits
▶ How to maintain momentum
▶ How to build name recognition and customer loyalty

Functioning as both a management tool and a communications device, your business plan provides a means for evaluating various growth strategies and for exchanging ideas and information. When used internally for decision-making purposes, the plan can help you to keep your business on track. When used externally as a sales aid, the plan can help you to win the support of lenders and investors.

A well-prepared and carefully thought-out plan is an invaluable business asset. By addressing the various aspects of growing a business, you are forced to examine your enterprise with an objective, critical eye; and by going through the process of developing a plan, you have a better grasp of what it will take to make your business succeed.

PREPARING A WINNING PLAN

To ensure that your business growth plan is the best it can be, you should approach the act of writing it as an exploration, rather than an exercise. Important as the plan is, the process of creating it is even more valuable. Instead of thinking of it as an unpleasant task or time wasted, it should be seen in a positive light and viewed as an opportunity to develop a better understanding of your business . . . and yourself.

You're not just putting words and numbers on paper, you're writing the scenario for your business as you would like it to unfold. This entails looking at everything that has a bearing on the business and seeing how each element comes into play—customers' needs, competitors' actions, financing alternatives, advances in technology, your own capabilities, and so on. The more information you're able to gather and the better you are at piecing it together, the more accurate your planning scenario will be.

The Key Ingredients

When it comes to the structure and content of your plan, there's no one format that must be followed. However, certain key ingredients, or sections, should be included—both for the information they provide for you and because lenders and investors expect to see them.

Your business growth plan should include the following information:

BUSINESS PLAN SECTIONS
- Title Page
- Table of Contents
- Executive Summary
- Business/Industry Profile
- Products or Services Description
- Sales and Marketing Information
- Competitive Analysis
- Management Structure
- Operations System
- Research and Development
- Financial Data

Title Page

Showing the name of your business, its address and telephone number, this page carries a greater weight than you might imagine, since it is the first thing that others see. It also serves the vital function of providing a means of contacting you. Other information that goes here is the date the plan was prepared, along with the owners' names and/or the chief executive officer's name. You may also want to show a copy number. The purpose of this is both practical and psychological; it enables you to keep track of the plans distributed and tells readers that they are among the few to see the plan since only a limited number of copies are in circulation.

Table of Contents

The table of contents not only provides a preview of what's to come, but makes it easy for readers to locate the sections they want to see. To further highlight key information and make it more accessible, it's a good idea to number the pages by *section,* rather than sequentially (i.e., 2-1 to 2-5; 3-1 to 3-7). This pinpoints the information with greater accuracy, while showing its relationship to the other parts of the plan.

Executive Summary

Quite possibly the most important *two* pages you'll ever write about your business, the executive summary is a critical part of your business growth plan. It can make the plan soar or bring it down. Charged with the task of stirring the interest of potential lenders or investors, the role of the summary is to get them to read the rest of the plan, while not taking more than two pages (the maximum acceptable length) to do it. To accomplish this, it must paint a detailed and compelling picture of your business, including the following:

1. Background and industry.
2. Products or services and what makes them unique.
3. Target market and strategies for reaching it.
4. Competitive advantages that will enable it to succeed.
5. Primary objectives—both short- and long-term.
6. Management capabilities.
7. Financial projections.
8. Capitalization needs.

A scant two pages may seem inadequate for such detail, but one way to get a handle on your summary is to *write it last.*

Even though it comes first in the plan, if you actually write the executive summary after you've completed everything else, you'll have a better idea of what to target and what to highlight for potential lenders and investors.

Business/Industry Profile

In this section, information about the founding of the business, its purpose, goals, and objectives should be included, as well as legal structure, subsidiary businesses or investments, location(s), and number of employees. It's also important to describe the industry in which your business operates, explaining who the key players are and the major changes that are occurring in it. Special attention should be given to any factors that make your business more appealing, such as growth potential, a positive industry image, minimal government regulation, and so on.

Products or Services

Picking up where the previous section left off, this section describes your products or services, highlighting how they're made and what makes them unique or superior to that of the competition. The specific *benefits* associated with using them should be emphasized here along with any proof you have that shows customer acceptance—marketing research data, sales figures, or testimonials. If you have an exclusive right to the products or services through patent protection or access to proprietary information, that should also be emphasized.

Sales and Marketing Information

Having a good product or service isn't enough. You must be able to sell it. The purpose of this section is to define the size, scope, and characteristics of your target market and the methods you will employ to get a larger share of it. In addition to describing who your customer is, you should also describe your overall marketing strategy—distribution and sales techniques, pricing, promotion, and publicity—as well as how you will expand and improve it.

Competitive Analysis

Since no business exists in a vacuum, it's important to know who your competitors are and how your products or services and marketing methods stack up against theirs. Looking at your strengths and weaknesses and those of other businesses in your field, your competitive analysis should point out the factors that will enable you to continue to compete successfully. For example, these might include: a better designed product, superior technology, lower cost structure, or a more efficient distribution network. Or perhaps you're avoiding the competition by focusing on a market niche that the other businesses have ignored. If so, this should be explained along with the advantages of going after that particular market. Again, testimonials, sales figures, and market research can be used here.

Management Structure

Having looked at the product side of your business, now it's time to look at the people side. How is your business organized? Who does what and reports to whom? In this section you should describe your management team, including *resumes, job descriptions,* and an *organization chart.* This is especially important if you're trying to raise capital, because lenders and investors want to know who they're trusting with their money. If you're currently going it alone and don't have partners or employees, be sure to emphasize the duties you will be performing and your background and qualifications. Information about any outside consultants or advisers you're working with should be included here along with your estimated personnel needs for expansion.

Operations System

This section of your plan focuses on your facilities, equipment, supplies, and inventory to show how your product or service reaches the consumer. In addition to providing an overview of your operation's system—production processes, personnel, quality and inventory control methods, handling and distribution—you also want to provide information about your relations with suppliers, subcontractors, and distributors. If you are utilizing new technologies or procedures that give you a competitive edge, be sure to underscore this advantage, and explain how they are superior. If you have discovered a way to streamline your operation, include that here as well.

Research and Development

What's in the pipeline? Are you currently working on anything new that you hope to market in the future? If you're involved in modifying existing products or services or in developing new ones, that should be spelled out here along with their cost and sales projections and the time required to complete the work. Other factors to note include the patentability of the new products and the extent to which they will make competing products obsolete.

Financial Data

This is the section of your plan that lenders and investors are likely to scrutinize the most closely, and it is where you must translate everything into dollars and cents—the all-important "bottom line." Calculating your estimated revenues and expenses, assets, and liabilities for the next three years, the information provided here should include *income statements, balance sheets,* and *cash flow projections,* as well as your financial statements for the past two years.

The question to answer is "Will the business be able to earn enough of a profit to justify being involved in it?" As an entrepreneur you need to know this because you will be putting more time, money, and energy into it; lenders need to know what the likelihood is of getting their money repaid; and investors need to know what rate of return to expect.

PUTTING YOUR PLAN TO WORK

Once you've put your plan in writing you're ready to tackle the real challenge—putting it to work. To get the most out of your business plan, you have to *use* it. Rather than filing it away or relegating it to a back shelf, it's important to keep it close at hand. You'll find the information in your growth plan can help you in such areas as the following:

• Organizing your business productively
• Raising capital when needed
• Assessing new opportunities
• Monitoring performance
• Managing your assets

Organizing Your Business Productively

Whether your business is just starting to take root or is already well established, your business growth plan can help you to organize it in the most productive way possible. By highlighting your goals and objectives and assessing your current capabilities, it can show you how to put your resources where they will do the most good. Rather than trying to move in opposite directions, you can use the plan to coordinate your growth strategies, focusing on:

▶ What needs to be done
▶ Who should do it

▶ How it should be accomplished
▶ When it should be completed

By showing the activities and events that need to take place—evaluating the market, producing the product, setting up sales territories, and so on—the plan shows both the steps to take and who must take them to get where you want to go.

Raising Capital

Attempting to raise capital to help your business grow without having a plan is like trying to run a marathon without shoes; it makes the task a lot harder. And, even if you do succeed, the results aren't likely to be as good as they could be. In most instances, lenders and investors won't even consider putting money into a business without seeing a business plan, no matter how enticing your current profits. Venture capitalists are particularly insistent about the need for a plan, often refusing to meet business owners if they haven't already submitted a plan or if the plan is not up to their standards. So, in a sense, your business plan is your ticket of admission to sources of financing as we will see in Chapter Three. The better the plan, the greater your access to capital.

Assessing New Opportunities

Your business growth plan can be especially useful in assessing new opportunities and making decisions about which products to develop or fields to enter. Providing an overall growth strategy and guidelines for utilizing your resources can help you to determine which opportunities are the most promising. That way there's less chance of wasting your time on something that isn't capable of generating sufficient profits or your getting involved in an area that you haven't researched adequately. If properly organized, a business growth plan will show you whether or not there is potential for expansion or if you need to reconsider your strategy.

Monitoring Performance

One of the most important uses of a business plan is as a control device. The goals and projections included in your plan provide bench marks that can be used to monitor your performance, telling you how far along you are in meeting your objectives. What are current sales levels? How many units are being produced? Which markets are you reaching? Are you ahead of plan, behind, or right on target? Which areas are performing better than expected and which are performing worse? By pinpointing the business's strengths and weaknesses, your plan can enable you to take quick action when necessary, as well as keep you from acting in the wrong areas.

Managing Your Assets

As your business grows, more time and attention will have to go into managing your assets. This includes not only such tangible assets as cash, accounts receivable, facilities, equipment, and inventory, but intangibles, too, such as patents, trademarks, and goodwill. By suggesting strategies for the best ways to utilize your assets, a plan can add to their value and help you to protect them against damage or loss.

GETTING OTHERS INVOLVED

Planning can't be delegated, but it can be *shared*. In fact, the best business plans are generally those that have had the benefit of more than one person's input. Getting others involved in the planning process has three advantages: (1) it elicits information that wouldn't otherwise be available; (2) it makes it easier to implement the plan later by gaining added support for it; and

(3) it shows your determination and continued enthusiasm for your venture.

Depending on your current situation and the reason for the planning effort—to launch a new venture, raise capital, update an existing plan, acquire another business, or for some other purpose—different inputs may be needed. Among the people entrepreneurs most often turn to for help in the planning process are:

► Partners
► Key executives
► Accountants
► Lawyers
► Bankers
► Company directors
► Outside advisers
► Planning consultants

There are also a number of computer software programs on the market that can provide planning assistance, helping you to format the material and prepare the financials.

Whatever sources of help you utilize, the main thing is to get in the planning habit. Planning isn't just something you do once and you're done with it. It's an ongoing process that must be carried out over the life of your business. To make sure that your business plan is adequately meeting your needs, experts generally recommend updating it every six to twelve months, and not just when you're contemplating growth or further development.

Planning is time-consuming and it can often seem like a tiresome chore. But it can also be a pleasure, providing new insights not only into your business, but into your reasons for being an entrepreneur.

2 | ESTABLISHING NEW GOALS

I n setting objectives for growing your business, it's absolutely essential to set your own personal objectives as well. What do you as an individual want? How do *you* want to grow? Will achieving the goals of the business enable you to achieve your personal goals, too? The saying, "Be careful what you wish for; you might *get* it," holds special meaning for entrepreneurs. To ensure that your business is able to satisfy your needs, rather than it forcing you to sacrifice them, it's important to chart your own personal course of action.

PERSONAL GROWTH OBJECTIVES

Growing a business requires a high level of commitment and determination along with lots of hard work. In making the decision to be "the boss" you're not only taking a risk, but taking on the responsibility for your own future. It stands to reason that you should give some serious thought to what you hope to gain; defining your objectives not only in terms of the money you want to make, but the life you want to lead.

Difficult as it may be, you must look within yourself and explore your own personal reasons for growing a business. Ask yourself, What's important to you? What do you want to accomplish? What needs do you want to fulfill—both personally and professionally? What must you have to consider yourself a success?

To help get started, use the Entrepreneur's Personal Objectives chart shown here to rate the things that matter to you.

ENTREPRENEUR'S PERSONAL OBJECTIVES

OBJECTIVES	VERY IMPORTANT	MODERATELY IMPORTANT	RELATIVELY UNIMPORTANT
1. To be creative	————	————	————
2. Personal achievement	————	————	————
3. Independence	————	————	————
4. Security	————	————	————
5. Meaningful work	————	————	————
6. To make a lot of money	————	————	————
7. Recognition from peers	————	————	————
8. Recognition from society	————	————	————
9. Recognition from family	————	————	————

OBJECTIVES	VERY IMPORTANT	MODERATELY IMPORTANT	RELATIVELY UNIMPORTANT
10. Time to myself	————	————	————
11. Time with my family	————	————	————
12. Low amount of stress	————	————	————
13. Intellectual growth	————	————	————
14. Adventure and excitement	————	————	————
15. Strong friendships	————	————	————
16. Prestige	————	————	————
17. Opportunity to travel	————	————	————
18. To meet new people	————	————	————
19. To be a leader in my industry	————	————	————
20. Involvement in civic activities and politics	————	————	————
21. Attain a high level of technical expertise	————	————	————
22. To have a stable environment	————	————	————
23. An affluent lifestyle	————	————	————
24. An active social life	————	————	————
25. Being attractive to others	————	————	————

OBJECTIVES	VERY IMPORTANT	MODERATELY IMPORTANT	RELATIVELY UNIMPORTANT
26. Being liked by others	_____	_____	_____
27. To develop my spiritual side	_____	_____	_____
28. To have leisure time	_____	_____	_____
29. To provide for retirement	_____	_____	_____
30. To improve society	_____	_____	_____

The more knowledgeable you are about your own needs, wants, goals, and interests, the better able you'll be to steer the business in the direction you want to go. By knowing what's important to you, you can seek out opportunities and situations that will help you to reach your personal objectives and avoid those that won't.

Thus, if you want to travel and learn about other cultures, one of the ways that you might expand your business is by entering foreign markets. On the other hand, if you need to have more control over your environment or want more time to spend with your family, you can focus on target markets closer to home. Or, if it's important to you to maintain a high level of technical expertise, you can position your business so that it's on the cutting edge of technology, rather than producing the same "me, too" products that everyone else makes.

The more in sync your personal objectives are with your business objectives, the better. This not only reduces points of conflict, but increases the likelihood that you *and* the business will succeed.

One Look Isn't Enough

Looking at your personal objectives and assessing your needs is something you need to do on a continual basis. In many instances, entrepreneurs do this in the beginning when their businesses are getting started and that's it. They don't think about it again . . . unless a crisis—either personal or business—comes up. And then they think about it a lot, asking themselves, "How did this happen?" "What did I do wrong?"

Without realizing it, entrepreneurs can find themselves doing work they no longer enjoy . . . or never did. This can be due to a shift in responsibilities, a change in the direction of the business, or any number of reasons. For example, the idea person suddenly discovers that somewhere along the way he or she was transformed into an administrator, spending more time on paperwork than on product development, behind a desk than at the drawing board.

It's also important to remember that as your business grows, its needs change and so do yours. Something that was once a high priority may no longer matter as much. For example, where money was once the driving force, it may have been supplanted by the desire to be an industry leader, to have more leisure time, or to help others.

In either case, it's time to take another look at the things that matter and set new personal objectives.

SKILLS AND PREFERENCES

In addition to looking at your personal objectives—what you want to be or accomplish—you should also look at your *skills* and *preferences;* the things you do best and enjoy the most. The more you're able to focus your attention on these areas, the more satisfied—and productive—you're likely to be.

For help in assessing your skills and preferences, use the chart shown below:

ENTREPRENEUR'S SKILLS/PREFERENCES EVALUATION

BUSINESS ACTIVITIES	SKILL		PREFERENCE	
	STRONG	WEAK	LIKE	DISLIKE
Administering	_____	_____	_____	_____
Representing the business	_____	_____	_____	_____
Creating	_____	_____	_____	_____
Performing technical duties	_____	_____	_____	_____
Thinking	_____	_____	_____	_____
Communicating	_____	_____	_____	_____
Interacting with others	_____	_____	_____	_____
Planning	_____	_____	_____	_____
Buying	_____	_____	_____	_____
Selling	_____	_____	_____	_____
Training employees	_____	_____	_____	_____
Motivating	_____	_____	_____	_____
Researching	_____	_____	_____	_____
Forecasting	_____	_____	_____	_____
Raising Capital	_____	_____	_____	_____

Once you've determined the activities that you're best suited to perform, you can use this knowledge to capitalize on your strengths and compensate for your weaknesses. This will not only put you in a better position to grow your business, but also to develop your potential.

GOAL-SETTING

Entrepreneurs who try to do everything at once or expect to become "overnight" successes are just setting themselves up for failure. To accomplish your personal objectives, it's important to set goals for yourself outlining the various steps that you must take to get where you want to go.

To achieve the best results, your goals should be as follows:

Specific. Picture in your mind exactly what you want to accomplish. The more specific and tangible you make your goals, the better your chance of reaching them. The most successful entrepreneurs are able to *see* their goals and to envision themselves doing the things that are necessary to attain them.

Measurable. In order to know when you've reached a goal, you must be able to recognize it. This means setting various milestones you can use to monitor your progress—dollars earned, types of work performed, knowledge gained, hours spent, etc. To say that you want to be "rich" or to "have control over your life" or to "help others" isn't enough. How *much* money do you want? In what *ways* do you want to be in control? *How* would you help others?

Realistic. Your goals should also be realistic. Having high aspirations is one thing, deluding yourself is another. In setting your goals, you need to take an objective look at your resources and capabilities and the current environment. Rather than setting impossible-to-reach goals and getting discouraged, it's better to set attainable goals and use them as springboards to your next goals.

Timed. To keep yourself moving in the right direction, you should establish a timetable for what you want accomplished, setting both short- and long-term goals. Then, when a goal is met, you can replace it with a new one. And if you fall behind schedule or your needs change, you can stop to analyze the situation and take the appropriate corrective action.

Written down. One of the surest ways to reach your goals is to write them down. This not only helps to fix them in your mind, but to keep them in perspective. That way you can see the relationships between the various things you want to accomplish and can also spot any conflicts between those that need to be resolved.

Reviewed. To ensure that you're actively pursuing the goals that are important to you, from time to time you should review them, updating and modifying them as needed. One of the reasons entrepreneurs are often reluctant to put their goals in writing is that they don't want to get locked into one course of action. But, this shouldn't be a problem if you make goal-setting an ongoing process of discovery, defining, and redefining your goals as your needs and circumstances change.

CHOOSING YOUR PATH

There's no one right way to grow a business. Growing a business is about making *choices*. First and foremost, your business has to be your own creation, reflecting your own dreams and desires and the choices that you make.

Rather than organizing your business to suit the latest management theories or trying to live up to others' expectations, you have to discover your own core values and mold the business to reflect them. Whether that means providing the best service, better value, greater access, or whatever, your priorities should be incorporated into your business. L. L. Bean built his mail-order empire on the notion that no sale was final until the customer said it was; and backed it up with an unconditional, no questions asked, money-back guarantee. Debbi Fields started with the premise that "good enough never is," combined it with her own chocolate chip cookie recipe, and turned it into Mrs. Fields Cookies.

As an entrepreneur, you must be open to new ideas and input and be willing to explore and experiment. That's part of the challenge—and the fun—of growing a business; but ultimately, you must be the one to decide what you want your business to be.

Some entrepreneurs prefer to grow "lifestyle" businesses structured around the things they do—independent consulting, photography, and so on—making their businesses extensions of themselves. Rather than measuring growth primarily in terms of size or revenue, they tend to measure it more by personal satisfaction in the work they are doing. Other entrepreneurs want to build something that stands the test of time, to turn an idea into a business that can provide employment to hundreds or thousands of workers.

Neither approach is right or wrong. It's a matter of what's right for you.

In his poem "The Road Not Taken," Robert Frost points out the importance of finding the right path to follow, noting that in his case, the choice "made all the difference."

The same is true in growing your business. There are many ways to succeed and many paths to follow; but to have success on your own terms, you must choose the path that is best for you.

3 | SHAKING THE MONEY TREE

Just as a plant can't grow without water, neither can a business grow without capital. Having access to money when you need it is essential for continued growth. In addition to raising the seed capital to get started, entrepreneurs must also know how to raise expansion capital to meet ongoing needs. For example, as a business evolves from one stage to the next (start-up, growth, maturity) money is important for several purposes, including the need to:

▶ Hire more employees
▶ Purchase additional equipment
▶ Expand facilities
▶ Add new locations
▶ Develop new products
▶ Increase promotional activities
▶ Gather marketing research data
▶ Acquire other businesses

Raising capital is probably one of the things entrepreneurs dread the most. It can be a frustrating and often humbling experience; but it doesn't have to be the ordeal that you might expect. Preparation is the key. By taking the time to develop a financing strategy that balances your needs with those of potential lenders or investors, you can strengthen your position and make your business more bankable.

DEBT VERSUS EQUITY

For starters, you must determine what kind of capital you want to utilize—debt, equity, or a combination of the two. *Debt capital* is money provided by lenders for a fee. *Equity capital* is money provided by investors in exchange for an ownership stake in the business. Neither type of financing is better than the other. It's a matter of what's best for you—in terms of the cost and availability of financing and the amount of control you must give up to obtain it.

Debt capital has these advantages and disadvantages:

ADVANTAGES
- Lenders do not receive any ownership in the business
- The cost of the loan is known in advance
- Interest payments can be deducted from your taxes
- Repayment of the loan terminates the financing relationship

DISADVANTAGES
- The loan must be repaid with interest
- Making payments may be difficult if revenues drop
- When interest rates are high the cost is expensive
- Lenders generally want some form of collateral

Equity capital has these advantages and disadvantages:

ADVANTAGES

- The money does not have to be repaid
- There is no fee for it
- It isn't necessary to put up collateral
- Investors can often provide nonfinancial support

DISADVANTAGES

- Investors receive ownership in the business
- Profits must be shared
- A portion of your control must be given up
- Dividends paid to investors are not tax deductible

In comparing the advantages and disadvantages of debt versus equity it's important to consider *why* you need the money. What is its intended purpose? to develop an employee training program or to buy out a competitor? If the money needed is just a small amount or only going to be used for a short period of time, it makes sense to use debt financing. On the other hand, if a large amount is needed over an extended period, then either equity financing or a long-term loan that gives you ample time to make repayment may be in order. As a rule of thumb, short-term capital should be used to finance short-term needs and long-term capital for long-term needs.

SOURCES OF FINANCING

There are a number of sources for business financing you can turn to, public and private, ranging from individual investors to large insurance and pension funds. Surprisingly, there's more money available for business start-up and expansion purposes than most people realize. But you have to know where to look for it . . . and what you will be expected to provide in return.

In addition to yourself, family members, and friends, here are other sources of financing that you should investigate:

- Banks
- Credit Unions
- Savings and Loan Associations
- Small Business Administration
- Small Business Investment Companies
- Business and Industrial Development Corporations
- Suppliers
- Factors
- Financing Companies
- Wealthy Individuals
- Partners
- Shareholders
- Bondholders
- Venture Capitalists
- Insurance Companies
- Pension Funds

Banks

The thing to remember in approaching a bank for a loan is that not all banks are the same. Some banks make a high percentage of business loans, others barely any at all or only to major corporations. To avoid hitting your head against the wall, you should check around—talking to other business people, your accountant or attorney—to find out which banks in your area are pro business. If possible, you should also try to find a bank that is familiar with your type of industry and the way it operates.

Once you've determined which banks to contact, you'll want to have your business plan and financial statements in order. Bankers, as a rule, tend to be cautious. Whereas entrepreneurs deal in dreams, bankers deal in debits and credits. No matter how good your ideas or intentions may be, bankers are going to want to see an income statement and other back-up information.

The higher you rate in what bankers call the "six C's of credit," the greater the likelihood of getting your loan approved. Each C—capital, collateral, capability, character, coverage, and circumstances—refers to a critical factor in granting a loan. Thus, in evaluating your loan request, bankers will be looking at your:

► Capital: The amount of money already invested in your business or available for future investment

► Collateral: The assets you own that could be used to secure the loan

► Capability: Your ability to repay the loan based on current and projected income flows

► Character: Your personal reputation and credit history

► Coverage: The insurance or safety precautions needed to protect the lender's investment

► Circumstances: Both the current financial situation of your business and the economy, as a whole

If deficiencies exist, rather than trying to hide them or hoping lenders won't notice them, be prepared to explain what you're doing to correct the problem areas and/or to point out the offsetting factors in your favor. Bankers *do* want to lend money, but it's up to you to demonstrate that you're a good risk. And if you get turned down, don't get discouraged; learn from the experience and go on. There are other banks and sources of financing who may feel quite differently about providing the capital you need.

Credit Unions
Although credit unions are set up to provide their members with short-term consumer loans and generally don't make business loans per se, if you just need a small amount of money,

they can still be a good source of business capital. For example, if your credit rating is good, you can probably qualify for a personal signature loan of up to $10,000. And now that computers are commonplace in many homes, credit unions are making computer loans as a matter of course. You may be able to obtain money for an automobile or furniture that can be used to expand your business, as well.

Since credit unions exist to serve their members, it's sometimes easier to get a loan from them. And their rates are often lower, so you can end up paying less for it.

Savings and Loan Associations
Another alternative to a bank is a savings and loan association (S&L). In recent years more and more S&Ls have moved beyond their traditional areas of home improvement and mortgage loans into general consumer and business loans. In an effort to counter any downturns in the housing market and avoid tying their money up in long-term loans, S&Ls have become increasingly receptive to making business loans for a variety of purposes. Not all S&Ls are as entrepreneurial as others, so you'll have to do some research to see which ones to approach.

Small Business Administration
If you're not able to obtain financing from a conventional lender, such as a bank or S&L, you should see what's available through the Small Business Administration (SBA). Established by the federal government for the purpose of providing entrepreneurs with business advice and financial assistance, the SBA oversees several loan programs. Calling itself the "lender of last resort," the SBA doesn't compete with lenders, but works *with* them. One way it does this is to guarantee loans for up to 90 percent of the loan amount, thus enabling banks to make loans that might otherwise be considered too risky. Another way, when

no other financing is available, is for the SBA itself to lend the money. But these *direct loans* are made only on a limited basis; borrowers must meet certain criteria, such as being a Vietnam-era veteran or physically handicapped, in order to qualify.

While the SBA is often willing to say yes when other lenders say no, it still expects to see a well-worked business plan and a full set of financials before it gives the go-ahead on a loan application. Generally, it also requires each entrepreneur to also put his or her own money into the business; a contribution of at least one-third of the total equity.

Small Business Investment Companies

Small Business Investment Companies (SBICs) are privately owned companies that are licensed and regulated by the SBA for the purpose of providing businesses with both equity capital and long-term loans. Functioning, by turns, as investor and lender, an SBIC can be a valuable business ally not only for its financial support but also for the information and management assistance it makes available. No two SBICs are alike. Some prefer to become partial owners in the businesses they assist; others focus primarily on making loans. There are also SBICs that specialize in certain industries, such as the garment indus-try or telecommunications field. So, just as with any other source of financing, you'll have to do some research to deter-mine which SBIC's needs and preferences coincide with yours.

Business and Industrial Development Corporations

Business and Industrial Development Corporations (BIDCOs) are similar to SBICs in that they are privately owned, for-profit corporations working with the SBA to provide entrepreneurs with capital. They operate at the state level and act only as lenders. Chartered by the Department of State Banking, they specialize in offering SBA-guaranteed loans to small businesses.

In addition to being familiar with entrepreneurs' money needs, they are often able to make loans that other lenders cannot.

Suppliers

One of your best sources of financing may not be a lender or investor at all, but your suppliers. If you've established a good relationship with them, they may be willing to provide you with capital or the next best thing, *trade credit,* enabling you to obtain inventory, furniture, equipment, and other items on a deferred payment basis. Offering extended payment plans ranging from thirty days to a year or more, suppliers are often willing to help a business when others won't, and for good reason: If the business continues to succeed, the supplier grows with the customer; if it fails, the supplier can repossess the items bought on credit.

Even if you don't need supplier credit, it's still a good idea to set up a trade account with your suppliers whenever possible, even when you first start your business. This makes it easier to pay for deliveries and keep track of purchases. Plus, any interest charges are tax deductible. And, by using trade credit, you're helping to build your credit rating.

Factors

Another, often overlooked, source of financing is a factoring service. As described in Chapter Fifteen, factors provide businesses with ready cash in exchange for their accounts receivable. The main advantage of factors is that they move quickly. And since the money received is a *payment,* not a loan or an investment, this method of raising capital doesn't entail taking on debt or sharing equity. Depending on what a factor's willing to pay, though, it can be costly. So, it's important to compare factoring services, to make sure you're getting top dollar for your accounts receivable.

Finance Companies

Like factors, finance companies can provide cash in a hurry. By approving loans that banks and other lenders have turned down, they take greater risks, but they also charge higher fees. In fact, their interest rates can be very steep. As a result, this source of financing should be used sparingly, with careful thought given to what the money will cost.

Wealthy Individuals

Wealthy individuals, often called *angels,* are becoming an increasingly utilized source of business financing. Sometimes operating alone and other times as part of investment groups, angels come in all shapes and sizes including: other entrepreneurs, doctors, lawyers, accountants, stock brokers, well-paid entertainers, and athletes. Some are just looking for a place to put their money where there is a high return on investment; others want to be actively involved in the businesses they support. Although providing both debt and equity financing, the majority of angels prefer equity since that gives them an ownership stake in the business.

If you want to find an angel, there are several ways to go about it. The best way is to obtain a referral from a mutual friend, relative, or business associate. Asking your accountant, banker, or stock broker for a lead is also a good idea; so is contacting your local chamber of commerce. Or you can place a classified ad in the "Business Opportunities" section of a newspaper or magazine. This offers the dual advantage of enabling you to branch out beyond your immediate circle of contacts and to reach many potential investors at once.

Before you enter into a relationship with anyone, take the time to find out as much as you can about each person who wants to invest in your business. Some angels turn out to be devils. You want to make sure that you're compatible with the people you let buy into your business; otherwise, you could end up paying more for the money than you intended.

Partners

Entering into a partnership agreement is another way to raise capital. Teaming up with other individuals or businesses with similar goals as yours can go a long way toward growing your business. Providing more than money, partners can enable you to accomplish objectives that wouldn't otherwise be possible. Choose your partners carefully, though. Compatibility is especially important here, since partners not only share in the ownership and profits of a business, but also in decision-making, and can be held legally responsible for one another's actions.

Shareholders

If your business is a corporation, then one obvious way to raise capital is by selling shares of stock either through private or public placements. This method is often necessary when large sums of money are needed for such purposes as funding ongoing research and development activities or implementing large scale expansion plans. To achieve maximum financial benefit, the size, price, and timing of the stock offering are critical. There are also the legal aspects to consider, along with the issue of management control. In focusing on the money to be gained, entrepreneurs sometimes lose sight of the fact that shareholders are entitled to a say in corporate decisions. To adequately assess this option, you'll need to get advice from financial experts. For more information on public stock offerings, see Chapter Twelve.

Bondholders

Another financing option open to corporations is to sell bonds. In this instance, rather than sharing equity, you are incurring long-term debt, borrowing money that must be repaid with interest in accordance with the terms of the bond. Bonds are generally issued with maturity dates of ten to thirty years. Throughout the life of the bond each bondholder receives a predetermined rate of interest until the bond fully matures, at which time the principal investment is repaid and the bond is retired.

The advantage of issuing bonds to raise capital is that you don't have to relinquish any management control and the interest payments are tax deductible. The money must be repaid eventually; so, to avoid running into financial problems later, it's important to make provisions in advance to have sufficient funds on hand when the bonds come due.

Venture Capitalists

Venture capital firms are an excellent source of financing for high-growth businesses with strong profit potential. Often specialized in an industry, such as telecommunications, computers, or health care, venture capitalists are always on the lookout for businesses they can help grow. They are extremely selective when it comes to choosing investment candidates, though. Like the marines, venture capitalists want only the "proud few" who can meet their strict criteria. Most important of all, the businesses must have the ability to grow large enough and fast enough to provide a high return on investment—typically 25 to 50 percent over a three- to seven-year period. Businesses that prefer a slower pace of growth or aren't willing to make a public stock offering would generally be viewed negatively.

Venture capitalists demand a lot, but they also *give* a lot—start-up and expansion capital, management expertise, and business contacts. In determining whether or not to pursue this financing avenue, you should look at the arrangement from both sides: the venture capitalist's and your own. What does the venture capitalist want? And equally important, what do *you* want?

Venture capitalists, as a rule, want businesses that have:

▶ Capable management teams with proven track records
▶ Innovative ideas or technology, preferably backed by patents
▶ Unique products or services that buyers want
▶ Strong business plans and competitive marketing strategies

Entrepreneurs, on the other hand, generally want to find a venture capital firm that will:

▶ Provide sufficient capital for their needs
▶ Offer expertise in those areas where they are lacking
▶ Assist them in making business contacts
▶ Leave the running of the business to them

Ultimately it comes down to this: Can you meet the venture capitalist's expectations and can the venture capitalist meet yours?

Insurance Companies

A source of financing that many businesses are unaware of is insurance companies. Known in the financial community as "hidden bankers," they often possess large sums of investment capital as a result of the insurance premiums they receive. Operating independently or through venture capital partnerships, insurance companies provide both debt and equity financing; or combining the two, sometimes they will agree to favorable loan terms in exchange for stock options.

Pension Funds

Employee pension funds are another source of financing that shouldn't be ignored. Functioning in much the same manner as insurance companies, they, too, have large sums of money available stemming from the retirement contributions made by the funds' members. Many of the state-run, public employee pension funds are particularly active in providing both start-up and expansion capital, often helping local and minority-owned businesses or those in high technology.

GETTING YOUR BANKER ON YOUR SIDE

The best way to get your banker on your side is to begin a relationship *before* you need money. The sooner, the better. Savvy entrepreneurs don't wait until it's time to ask for a loan to set up a meeting. They do it as early as the planning stage and keep the banker informed of their progress each step of the way as the business grows. That way when you *do* need money, instead of just being another name on a loan application, you'll be someone the banker knows.

How you view your banker is just as important as how the banker views you. For example, entrepreneurs who think of a banker as just someone to go to in an emergency or as someone who rubber-stamps loan applications aren't fully utilizing the banker's expertise. Worse yet, they're missing out on the opportunity to gain a strong advocate for their businesses. In addition, bankers can help you by providing financial advice and services, investment contacts, and vital business information. Even in those instances where they're not in a position to make a loan themselves they may still be able to assist you in raising the capital from other sources. So, it's to your advantage to think of them in multidimensional terms, rather than merely as loan processors. Therefore, look for a banker who has the combination of resources, knowledge, and temperament to match your needs.

Finding someone you feel comfortable working with is the

first step. After that it's up to you to then establish and maintain a positive banking relationship. Some of the things you can do to accomplish this include:

▶ Providing the banker with quarterly financial statements
▶ Providing marketing updates and information on new products or services
▶ Explaining what makes your business unique
▶ Discussing expansion plans in advance and asking for advice
▶ Being open and candid about any problems you are facing
▶ Inviting the banker to your place of business so that he or she can *see* what you're doing
▶ Showing respect for the banker's time and expertise
▶ Demonstrating through your actions that you are a responsible and ethical person
▶ Being enthusiastic about your business and its prospects— enthusiasm is contagious!

The stronger relationship you're able to build, the more you can count on having your banker's help when you need it. Communication is essential; to get your banker on your side you have to open the door.

QUESTIONS TO EXPECT

Before meeting with potential lenders or investors, you should be prepared to answer any and all questions about yourself, your business, and your finances. Among the questions to expect are:

▶ How much money do you need?
▶ What is the purpose of the funds?

▶ How and when will you make repayment?
▶ What collateral do you have?
▶ What is your professional background?
▶ How long have you been in business?
▶ What kind of business is it?
▶ What are your current and projected sales?
▶ Can you provide complete financial statements?
▶ Can you provide copies of your tax returns?
▶ How much of your money is in the business?
▶ Who else has put money into the business?
▶ What's its legal structure?
▶ Do you have a business plan?
▶ Are you on track in meeting your goals?
▶ Who's your target market?
▶ Who's your competition?
▶ Are you developing any new products or services?
▶ What are your expansion plans?
▶ Who are the key members of your management team?
▶ What do you want to accomplish in the next five to ten years?
▶ How would the business continue if something happened to you?

When it comes to shaking the money tree, the more information—backed up by facts and figures—that you're able to provide, the better the response you'll get. And, if you've kept your business plan current, the answers to most of these questions will be at your fingertips.

4

BUILDING
YOUR
TEAM

Successful entrepreneurs do more than grow businesses; they grow teams—recruiting the best people they can find and getting them to work together as a cohesive unit. Instead of thinking in terms of a single job opening or an immediate need, they look beyond that, thinking of the business organization as a whole and what its future needs will be.

To respond to the challenges ahead and keep your business moving forward, each worker that you choose must complement the others and be capable of developing new skills and taking on more responsibility as the situation calls for it. Finding the right people is crucial; and in making your choices, much like a baseball manager deciding whether to sign a player, you must consider the entire lineup, not just the position.

SCOUTING THE FIELD

The key to finding the people you need is knowing what to look for; not only the technical skills a job applicant should have, but also other characteristics, such as enthusiasm, a willingness to work, the ability to get along with others, and so on. It's important to realize that each business environment is different and that an employee who would be ideal in one situation might have difficulty in another. For example, someone who's used to working in a large, bureaucratic organization with several layers of management might not function well in a small, start-up operation, where everyone communicates face-to-face instead of going through channels. On the other hand, that same person could be just what the doctor ordered if your business is expanding rapidly and needs someone to bring order out of chaos, instituting procedures and controls to keep everything running smoothly.

In adding members to your team you should take into consideration:

- The work to be done
- The skills that are needed
- The level of responsibility involved
- The people that person will work with
- The work environment
- The changes occurring in your business

The work to be done. Are you looking for someone to produce your product or to sell it? To perform manual tasks or run the office? Program a computer or plan an ad campaign?

The skills that are needed. Is it important for the person to be good with words? Numbers? Does the job entail working with certain equipment or knowing how to carry out specific procedures—operating a forklift or processing escrow papers?

The level of responsibility involved. How important is the position to the achievement of your goals? Will the person have authority over others? Be involved in planning and decision making? Represent you or act on your behalf?

The people that person will work with. How many people are there? What background and experience do they have? What kinds of skills? How do they interact with one another?

The work environment. Is it fast-paced or slow? Casual or formal? Will the person be at one location or in the field? Working in an office or on the production floor? Coming into contact with customers or staying behind the scenes?

The changes occurring in your business. Is the job likely to grow or shrink? Become more administrative? Require more technical skills or stay the same? Involve more interaction with others or less?

By examining these factors, you ought to be able to get a clear picture of what the job entails and what attributes a person would need to fill it. For example, someone applying for a job as a salesperson for the busy Christmas season would need good communications skills and the ability to function in a fast-paced work environment. If the applicant has previous sales experience or a knowledge of the product being sold, so much the better.

Job Descriptions

Personnel experts recommend creating job descriptions outlining the duties and responsibilities for each position in your business. That way, when a new job is created or an opening comes up, you can compare the applicants to the description, looking for the best match.

A job description should include the following items:

- ▶ Job title: The position and its level
- ▶ Supervisor: Person to whom employee reports
- ▶ Job description: Brief summary of the work to be performed
- ▶ Major duties and responsibilities: Listed by priority
- ▶ Other duties: List of duties not performed on a regular basis
- ▶ Job specifications:
    Formal education or training required
    Experience or background required
    Skills necessary to carry out the work
- ▶ People supervised: Number

The use of job descriptions not only makes it easier for you to focus on the skills and abilities needed for a specific job, but it lets you see how each job fits together in your business— who's responsible for what, where duties and responsibilities overlap, where there are gaps. By reviewing the job descriptions and comparing them, you can identify strengths and weaknesses and eliminate points of conflict. The larger your work force gets, the more important it is to have an overview of the various positions within it. To get the most out of your team, you have to know who's on the bench and what they can do.

RECRUITING

Equally important as knowing what to look for in a job applicant is *where* to look. One of the common mistakes that entrepreneurs make in recruiting workers is failing to cast a wide enough net. They place a "help wanted" sign in the window or run an ad in the classifieds and that's it. The problem with limiting yourself to these methods is that it puts you in the position of passively waiting for people to contact you, rather than taking the initiative and actively seeking them out. Furthermore, it presupposes that the right people will see your notices and respond, when in fact they may not. To ensure that you're reaching the most suitable people, you must be aware of the various recruitment sources available and know which ones to use in each hiring situation.

Recruitment Sources

Some of the most frequently used recruitment sources include:

Employment agencies. Employment agencies (both public and private) will carry out the recruitment process for you, screening applicants, checking references, and determining which people are most qualified for the positions to be filled. Public agencies, which are state-operated, perform these services for free. Private agencies charge a fee.

Newspaper classifieds. If you want to reach as many people as possible in a short period of time, this is the way to go. The newspaper's circulation and the size and frequency of your advertisement will determine how many people you reach. For maximum effectiveness, be sure to place the ad under the correct heading, so the people you want to see it can find it. Or you might list it in more than one section. For example, a job opening for a computer trainer might be listed under "Computers-Training" and "Training-Computers." The drawback of using newspaper classifieds is that the burden is on you to screen out the qualified from the unqualified applicants. Also, you may generate more telephone calls and inquires than you want. One way to avoid this is to run a *blank ad,* in which you omit the name and address of your business and use a post-office box instead.

School placement services. High school and college place-ment centers can be particularly helpful if you're seeking to fill an entry-level position or looking for part-time workers. If you wish, the centers may even assist you in establishing a student internship program, helping you to find students who will work for free in exchange for the opportunity to gain experience in your field.

Trade and professional associations. Consultants, special-ists, and other management-level personnel can often be found through the associations that represent their areas of expertise. For example, the computer trainer mentioned above might be reached through the Independent Computer Consultants Asso-ciation or the American Society of Training Directors.

Executive search firms. Executive search firms (also known as "headhunters") specialize in finding and placing high-level personnel, such as company presidents, chief financial officers, division and department heads, and the like. With extensive contacts and the resources to find qualified job candidates wherever they may be, executive search firms can be especially helpful to the growing business.

Unions. Unions are another recruitment source you can use if you're seeking licensed professionals or skilled craftspersons. Unions maintain rosters of qualified workers available for hire and will assist you in filling your employment needs.

Current employees. Your current employees can be one of your best recruitment sources of all. Rather than going outside your business to fill a job opening, whenever possible try to fill it by promoting from within. This approach has several advan-tages: (1) it reduces employee turnover by giving employees somewhere to go rather than out, (2) it motivates employees, (3) it cuts down on training time, and (4) it reduces your risk since you already know what the employee can do.

Referrals. Employees, business colleagues, and friends may send job applicants your way, too. What's more, since the quality of the applicant reflects on them, they're likely to think carefully before making a recommendation; in effect, part of the screening has already been done for you. The more you respect the judgment of the person giving the referral, the better the odds that you will be pleased with the job applicant.

Job applications and resumes. Job applications on file and unsolicited resumes that have been sent to you should also be checked. Because you didn't need the person when the application or resume first came in doesn't mean that the person wouldn't be perfect for your business now. Rather than starting from scratch to find new applicants, it makes sense to look through your files and reconsider those people who have already expressed an interest in working for you.

Depending on your business's stage of development and the types of positions to be filled, you'll find some of these recruitment sources work better than others. The main thing is to keep an open mind. No single recruitment source can possibly meet all your needs. And sources that worked in the past may no longer be effective. So it's important to not limit your options.

TRAINING

A winning team needs more than talent. It needs training. Contrary to what many business owners think, training isn't something only big businesses need to do. It's something all businesses must do, regardless of size; businesses that train better perform better.

You can't expect workers to meet tomorrow's goals with yesterday's capabilities. In order for your business to grow, your people must grow, becoming more proficient at their jobs and acquiring the necessary skills and confidence to move up into more challenging ones. Employee growth doesn't happen by accident. It happens by design—with the training and guidance that only you can provide.

Training Methods

There are a number of training methods you can use to help employees maintain or upgrade their skills and build confidence. As you will see from the methods that follow, they all have a common goal: to make employees more productive so that your business can compete effectively in the marketplace.

Vestibule training. Vestibule, or "entryway," training occurs *before* an employee assumes his or her regular duties. Conducted away from the actual work area, this training involves teaching workers how to use equipment or carry out procedures so that once they start work they can perform their jobs safely and competently.

On-the-job training. The most commonly used type of training, this method consists of having the employee learn by doing, gaining skills by watching others and then performing the work. For the best results, the trainee's progress should be closely monitored and suggestions made for improvement.

Apprenticeship. A more structured type of on-the-job training, this method is primarily used in the skilled crafts and trades—plumber, electrician or carpenter, for example. It entails having workers go through a series of steps, which can take years, during which they learn the skills of their trade and eventually earn the rank of journeyman.

Mentoring. One of the least expensive, but most effective, ways to train employees is by mentoring; matching a new employee with an experienced worker who can serve as a guide, or mentor, helping the employee to adjust to the work environment and develop needed skills. If your business is small or the situation warrants it, you may want to assume the role of mentor yourself. Mentoring is the fastest way for an employee to learn the ropes and feel a part of your business. And the mentors themselves benefit, gaining a sense of pride from being able to share what they've learned with someone else.

Job rotation. Job rotation, also referred to as "cross training," involves having workers perform different jobs on a rotating basis so that they learn additional skills. This not only gives you the flexibility to move workers into other positions when needed—to fill in for workers who are ill or on vacation—but benefits workers as well, by relieving boredom and opening up new career possibilities.

Classes and seminars. Classes and seminars can teach employees basic skills, such as word processing or equipment handling, or help prepare them for leadership positions by covering various management topics. A good source of classroom training is the colleges and universities in your community. You'll often find that they will even customize their courses to meet your needs. You should also check with your local chamber of commerce or Small Business Administration office to see what classes or seminars they offer. Another alternative is to provide your own classes, with yourself or an employee to teach them, or with an independent consultant to do the training.

Electronic training. More and more businesses are turning to interactive video/computer programs to provide the training that employees need. Utilization of personal computers or videodisc technology can create learning exercises that simulate the real work environment—giving a sales presentation, assembling a product. It also have the advantage of letting employees learn at their own speed and when it fits their work schedules.

Whatever training methods you use—informal or formal, hands-on or high-tech—it's important to create an environment where people can continue to learn and develop new skills. The time and effort you put into this won't be wasted. The opposite is true: The more you train, the more you gain.

DEVELOPING IN-HOUSE TALENT

Choosing your workers well and providing ongoing training are critical components of team building. At the same time, you must also help employees to focus their careers in directions that will be mutually beneficial. This means not only looking at what workers can do when they are hired, but what they can do down the road when both they and the business have grown.

To keep employees from languishing in their jobs and to assure yourself of having the bench strength you need to carry out your objectives, it's imperative that you (1) *Hire up,* choosing employees who are capable of working one or two levels up from the positions being filled, and (2) *Establish career tracks,* showing employees where they can go in your business and what steps they must take to get there.

By hiring up, you can take care of your current personnel needs while preparing for the future. Since higher-level jobs are more difficult to fill, hiring up provides you with a pipeline of qualified workers ready to move up. In addition to keeping your growth momentum going, this results in shortened learning periods for employees to adjust to their new jobs.

For hiring up to be effective, though, employees must know that they are being groomed to accept more responsibility and be aware of the career tracks open to them. It's easy for businesses to say, "We promote from within," but much more difficult to actually do it. Developing in-house talent takes time and a willingness on your part to help employees find and follow the career tracks most suited for them. It's not just a matter of moving employees into higher slots. It's moving them into the *right* slots . . . or sometimes not moving them at all.

As the following career tracks show, advancement can come in many forms and "growth" and "promotion" are not always the same:

Traditional career track. Based on gaining promotions, it calls for employees to move upward through the managerial ranks.

Parallel career track. This is for professionals and technical specialists (accountants, engineers, scientists, mechanics, etc.) who want to develop their skills, but aren't interested in moving into management. The track lets them earn more responsibility and pay while working in their chosen fields.

Horizontal career track. This track enables employees to make sideways moves into other areas that appeal to them or offer greater opportunities for upward mobility. Moving horizontally not only gets employees out of "dead end" jobs, but helps them to avoid "burnout" by giving them the opportunity to learn something new.

Status quo career track. A status quo career track essentially lets employees advance while staying in place. A contradiction in terms? Not at all. Instead of moving into new jobs, employees *enlarge* their current ones, upgrading their skills *and* their jobs, resulting in personal growth for the employees and productivity growth for your business.

FORGING A CORPORATE CULTURE

One of the most important aspects of team-building is to forge a corporate culture, instilling in workers a common purpose and a shared set of values. You want each team member to know what your business stands for and its approach to achieving its objectives and satisfying customers, especially during growth stages. Consisting of attitudes, ethical standards, and more, a corporate culture can be difficult to define or describe, but its presence is immediately felt; it is the unifying force that brings people together and guides their efforts. The stronger and more positive the corporate culture, the more the business can accomplish, and the faster your growth plans will be realized.

One has only to look at IBM and Apple to see the role a corporate culture has in shaping a business. The contrast between the two cultures was especially pronounced during the 1980s when the two companies began competing with each other in the personal computer market. The IBM culture was all business, reliable and practical, approaching the task of meeting the customer's needs from an engineer's viewpoint with white shirt and knotted-tie seriousness. Apple, on the other hand, took a more playful approach to satisfying the customer, putting the emphasis on being creative and finding alternative, "user-friendly" ways to solve problems (i.e., using a mouse to input data, rather than the keyboard). Whereas Apple commercials showed computer users getting an idea and rushing to the computer to implement it, IBM's commercials showed users in a boardroom collectively engaged in strategic planning. Apple's culture emphasized the individual; IBM's the team.

Since both companies were successful the distinctions may not seem to matter. In reality, they are very important. This is because a corporate culture sets the tone for how a business does things, sending a message to workers about which types of behavior are acceptable and what skills will be rewarded.

The time to begin forging your corporate culture is when you begin building your team, defining and redefining it as your business grows. Don't let the name fool you. Your business doesn't have to be a corporation or have a lot of workers to have a corporate culture. All businesses have one whether they realize it or not. Some are good and some are bad. The difference between a good and a bad corporate culture is that a good one inspires and energizes workers while a bad one does just the opposite, robbing them of ideas and initiative. The best corporate cultures generate employee loyalty and a strong commitment to customer service. The worst generate apathy and a disregard for the customer.

So, how can you make sure that *your* corporate culture fits into the first category? There are *three* things you can do:

1. **Create a corporate credo** stating your beliefs on how the business should be run, and the underlying principles that will guide it (honesty, fairness, and responsibility, among others). This doesn't have to be lengthy. Depending on what you want to say, a sentence may be enough, or a paragraph or a

page. The more clearly and concisely you can make your statement, the greater the impact your credo will have.

2. **Establish a code of ethics** outlining the ethical standards employees will be expected to uphold and the types of conduct that are acceptable and unacceptable. Among typical subjects included in a code of ethics are:

▶ Honesty
▶ Legal responsibilities
▶ Loyalty/conflict of interest
▶ Privacy issues
▶ Restrictions on insider trading
▶ Nondiscrimination policies
▶ Marketing practices
▶ Supplier relations
▶ Gift-giving/receiving
▶ Adherence to safety standards
▶ Outside activities

3. **Practice what you preach.** Your corporate culture will evolve as much (or more) from what you do as from what you say. For example: stating that your business is "an innovative company" won't make it so if employees are penalized for trying new ideas that don't work out.

For the best results, you should think of your corporate culture as a work in progress. A good corporate culture is dynamic, not static, changing over time to adapt to the needs of the business and its environment.

REWARDING TEAM MEMBERS

To keep the members of your team happy and productive, their efforts must be rewarded; employees should be compensated adequately and fairly. Taking into consideration your resources and the standards for your industry, pay scales, bonuses, benefits, etc. need careful thought.

Although every compensation plan is different, the most effective ones are designed to:

1. **Pay for performance,** ensuring that the more workers produce, the more money they can make.
2. **Reward everyone, not just a few,** ensuring that each worker gets an opportunity to participate in incentive programs—to earn a bonus, win a contest, etc.
3. **Maintain sales momentum,** ensuring that employees stay focused on their goals by providing interim rewards throughout the year, rather than just at year-end.
4. **Increase profitability,** ensuring that the costs of the plan are offset by higher revenues and an improved "bottom line."
5. **Enhance employee satisfaction,** ensuring that workers have a high level of commitment to the business.

Designing an employee compensation plan isn't just a matter of plugging in numbers and coming up with dollar amounts. The human element (workers' needs, wants, goals) must be factored in with the financial one. And, it helps to remember that the real issue isn't always pay, but *perception.*

Two workers can earn the same amount of money and one can feel underpaid while the other feels overpaid. One perceives the salary as meager; the other perceives it as substantial. What this tells you is that part of a compensation plan's effectiveness stems from how you present it. In building your team, workers must not only be paid adequately, but *think* that they are.

5 MOTIVATING YOURSELF AND OTHERS

As your team begins to take shape, one of your primary concerns should be motivation. From the first new hire on, you must continually devise effective ways to keep your employees—and yourself—motivated. The growth of your business and the level of success that it achieves is directly related to your own success as a motivator.

The people you rely on to help carry out the functions of your business, in turn, rely on you. As the owner, you are expected to provide leadership and to assist employees in their personal development. In addition to providing employees with a place to work, you must provide the guidance, support, and incentives that bring out their best efforts. Most important of all, you must find a way to share your vision for the business with them so that they can make it their own and work with you to turn it into a reality.

IT STARTS WITH YOU

Before you can motivate someone else you must first motivate yourself. Surprisingly, business owners are often unaware of their own motivational needs or downplay their importance. The general feeling is that just being the boss ought to be motivation enough; and in the beginning it is. Getting a business started and seeing it take root would give anyone an adrenaline rush. But once the initial excitement wears off, what can you do? At that point it's critical for you to discover new ways to maintain your energy level and enthusiasm, to keep the entrepreneurial spark alive. Otherwise you'll quickly find invention giving way to routine, brainstorming to bureaucracy, and the business that you put so much of yourself into suddenly drained of its vitality.

How can this be avoided? By becoming a *self-motivator* and identifying and seeking out those rewards that will spur you on to greater achievements. Among the things most often cited by entrepreneurs as motivators are:

- Being creative
- Problem-solving
- Learning
- Having control
- Acquiring wealth
- Accomplishing something
- Making a difference

Being Creative

One of the greatest joys in life is the opportunity to be creative, to use your skills and talents to freely express yourself. In the quest for greater revenues it's important not to lose sight of your creative side. Rather than falling into the trap of "business as usual," you must allow yourself to explore new options, invigorating both your business and yourself in the process.

Problem-Solving

The satisfaction that comes from finding the solution to a problem confronting your business or your customers can be a strong motivator. To grapple with a problem and to come up with a solution that's different and fresh—and right on target— is a reward in itself, separate from the amount of money it brings in. It forces you to stretch and grow. By putting your wits to the test, it also keeps complacency from setting in.

Learning

Learning itself can be a motivator. The most highly motivated and successful entrepreneurs are those who never stop learning. They learn from everything. Not just from their successes, but from their failures. Thomas Edison, whose entrepreneurial skills rivaled his inventive ones, tried more than a thousand times to invent the light bulb before he got it right; yet he became more motivated than ever. As he put it, "I didn't fail more than a thousand times trying to invent the light bulb. I learned more than a thousand different ways it wouldn't work."

Having Control

The desire to have control over what you do and how you spend your time is probably one of the things that motivated you to start your business. Entrepreneurs don't just go along for the ride. They get behind the wheel and drive the car. If you aren't careful, though, your business could end up controlling you. To stay in the driver's seat (and stay motivated) it's essential for you to have clearly defined and realistic business objectives, to know your own abilities and those of your employees, and to have an action plan for utilizing your resources.

Acquiring Wealth

The profit motive and the ability to acquire wealth through your own independent efforts is the cornerstone on which the free enterprise system is built. Setting financial goals for your business and yourself will not only keep you motivated, but will keep your business headed in the right direction. It's important that the goals be your own, though, and not someone else's. You must decide how much money you want to make, what personal possessions you want to have, and what kind of lifestyle you want. The constant push to acquire more wealth can actually be a demotivator if it keeps you from pursuing more interesting (but less lucrative) business projects or from having a life outside of work.

Accomplishing Something

Taking an idea and turning it into a successful business is a major accomplishment. What an artist does with paint or a writer does with words an entrepreneur does with the *factors of production* (land, labor, capital, and technology), combining them into his or her creation—the business. In addition to the accomplishment of establishing the business, there are other accomplishments that go with it: satisfying your customers, developing new products, improving quality, raising profits, and so on. Rather than letting these accomplishments slip by without notice, you owe it to yourself to savor them. Acknowledging what you've done and taking joy from that is what makes being an entrepreneur so worthwhile and what will give you the motivation to go on to the next step.

Making a Difference

Many entrepreneurs say that one of the things that motivated them to start their businesses and keeps them going is the opportunity to make a difference. To make a product the way you think it should be made, to serve customers' needs that are being ignored, to change people's lives for the better, or even to change the world. The entrepreneurs behind Ben and Jerry's ice cream are examples of this—turning out uniquely delicious flavors of ice cream like Chunky Monkey Banana Fudge and donating part of the profits they make to such worthy causes as saving the Amazon Rain Forest. Being able to use your business like this to help others can be one of the best motivators of all—for you *and* your employees.

MAKE YOUR DREAM *THEIR* DREAM

The first step you must take toward motivating your employees is to share your dream for the business with them and show how your dream can be their dream. It all comes down to "inclusion." The more employees feel included in what you're doing, the more committed they will be to helping you accomplish it.

Your employees must feel that when the business succeeds, they succeed. Rather than working for you, they're working *with* you, side by side in a win-win situation where everyone benefits.

For this to happen, though, you must communicate to employees the goals and mission of the business, what you want it to become (a scientific research laboratory or a pharmaceuticals giant?), their roles in bringing that about, and what they stand to gain from its success. The better you are at putting your dream into words and giving it a form that employees can see and identify with, the stronger their response will be. The dream can't be yours alone. To get the support you need to grow your business, everyone must believe in it.

WHAT DO WORKERS WANT?

To many business owners the answer to that is simple—money. Preferably a lot of it, they would tell you. And money *is* a motivator. But only one of many motivators. The things that workers want are as varied as the workers themselves, running the gamut from satisfaction to security, interaction with others to independence.

Rather than focusing on the size of employees' paychecks, you must consider the whole range of motivators available to you and find the ones that will work best with each individual.

Among the motivators workers most frequently list as being important to them are such incentives as the following:

- ▶ Meaningful work
- ▶ Recognition
- ▶ Responsibility
- ▶ Fringe benefits
- ▶ Job security
- ▶ Job training
- ▶ Good income
- ▶ Promotion opportunities
- ▶ Supportive coworkers
- ▶ Minimal stress
- ▶ Flexible hours
- ▶ Pleasant working conditions
- ▶ Independence
- ▶ Freedom of expression
- ▶ Praise
- ▶ Respect
- ▶ Status
- ▶ Personal growth
- ▶ Sense of achievement
- ▶ Fair company policies
- ▶ Open communications

With so many incentives to choose from, how do you know which ones to use? Fortunately, it doesn't take a crystal ball to figure it out, just your own observations. By getting to know your employees as individuals and finding out what their needs and concerns are, you should be able to determine what is most important to them. For instance, an employee who has recently gone back to school or had a child may be motivated by a flexible work schedule, while another employee, who's saving to buy a house, wants a raise or a promotion. Someone with a strong need for achievement may crave additional responsibility and recognition. People who are creative, on the other hand, should jump at the chance to express themselves. The challenge is to match the right incentive with the right employee.

Don't worry about trying to compete with the salaries and benefits that the major corporations offer. In all likelihood you can't. But there are other things you have to offer that they don't. To name a few: a collegial work environment where everyone knows each other, broader responsibilities and fewer restrictions, the opportunity to get in on the ground floor of a growing business, the chance to *start* company traditions rather than just follow them.

More important than the money you have to spend on incentives is the effort you put into letting employees know that they are appreciated and into making your business a place where people want to work. Taking the time to praise employees, showing an interest in them, and even making the workplace fun can go a long way toward motivating your team.

Charles Dickens illustrated this point very well in *A Christmas Carol*. Remember the party scene at Fezzwig's, Ebenezer Scrooge's former employer? Upon seeing his younger self dancing and laughing, Scrooge tells the Ghost of Christmas Past that the happiness Fezziwig gives his employees "is quite as great as if it cost a fortune." He explains that Fezziwig "has the power to render us happy or unhappy; to make our service light or burdensome; a pleasure or a toil. His power lies in words and looks; in things so slight and insignificant that it is impossible to add and count them up."

What was true of business owners in Dickens' time is no less true today. Often it's the so-called "little" things that mean so much to workers.

Keeping this in mind, some of the incentives—both large and small—you can use to motivate employees and build morale include:

▶ Treating employees with respect and fairness.

▶ Listening to employees.

▶ Leading by example.

▶ Bringing in donuts, bagels, or other treats from time to time.

▶ Holding "TGIF" pizza fests on Fridays so employees have a chance to mingle. This has become a tradition at the high-tech companies nestled in California's Silicon Valley.

▶ Having a Dress-Down Day or Crazy T-Shirt Day every so often to relieve tension.

▶ Giving employees awards or gifts for outstanding achievements. These needn't be expensive. Certificates, trophies, desk accessories, flowers, tickets to sporting events, dinner for two, or candy make thoughtful gifts.

▶ Holding a contest where employees who sell or produce the most have a chance to win a trip, watch, camera, electronics equipment, or other prize.

▶ Taking employees out to lunch.

▶ Picking an Employee of the Month and giving that person special recognition or VIP privileges.

▶ Giving a day off with pay.

▶ Writing thank you notes or letters.

▶ Telling employees they did a good job. Praise is one of the most powerful motivators of all . . . and it doesn't cost anything.

▶ Hosting a special event—a party, picnic, dinner, or day at an amusement park—and taking pictures of everyone having a good time. The pictures can be displayed for all to see and the happy memories will linger for months to come.

▶ Giving employees their own business cards. This raises self-esteem and also adds to the pride employees feel about working for you.

▶ Having T-shirts or caps imprinted with the name of your

business and giving them out to employees. The benefit of this is two-fold: increasing employees' identification with the business and keeping your name in public view.

▶ Awarding bonuses based on the business's profits.

▶ Offering shares of stock or stock options. These not only reward employees, but build loyalty by giving them a stake in the business.

▶ Paying a portion of employees' tuition costs if they attend college or obtain job-related training to upgrade skills.

▶ Offering employees discounts on your products or services.

▶ Setting aside time for employees to work on self-designated projects. This not only reduces burnout, but can benefit your business. For example, the Post-it note was invented by a 3M company employee working on an independent project.

▶ Giving raises or promotions.

▶ Making sure that meetings are productive, rather than just time wasters that keep employees from performing their jobs.

▶ Having a suggestion box . . . and encouraging employees to *use* it; and when an idea is implemented, rewarding the employee who suggested it.

▶ Having an open-door policy and being accessible when employees need to talk to you.

▶ Keeping employees updated on the business's progress and on those matters that are of concern to them—sales levels, personnel changes, new products or procedures, and so on.

▶ Making employees partners in the business. A time-honored practice in the professions and trades, this is a way to keep valued employees from going to another business.

▶ Sponsoring a company sports team.

▶ Sending flowers when employees get married or have a baby.

▶ Responding quickly to employees' complaints or problems.

▶ Giving support, rather than blame, when employees make mistakes or fail to meet a goal. The message you want to send is that the important thing is to try.

▶ Providing employees with a feeling of community and a place to belong.

▶ Giving employees a sense of purpose. The more important they believe their jobs are, the harder they will work at them.

Each business is different, of course, so obviously some of these methods will be more appropriate for you than others; and certain ones may not work at all. The point is to find the incentives that *will* work. To serve their purpose, the incentives you choose must not only fulfill the needs of individual employees, but of your business, as well.

MAINTAINING HIGH MORALE

To keep employees motivated and feeling good about their jobs, it's essential that you know how to recognize low morale when you see it and take action to reverse it. This isn't always easy; unlike sales volume or the amount of money paid out in commissions, morale can't be directly measured. Inasmuch as it's a state of mind or attitude, it can only be measured by observing employees' behavior.

As shown in the following chart, when employees have low morale they are likely to behave in ways that result in the following:

WARNING SIGNS OF LOW MORALE
- Increased absenteeism
- Reduced productivity
- Increased complaints
- High employee turnover
- Reduced product quality
- Frequent tardiness
- High accident rates
- Inadequate employee feedback

By being alert to these warning signs, you should be able to get a pretty good idea of whether morale is high or low. However, measuring morale and raising it are two different things. If low morale is detected, to correct it you must first determine the *problems* that are causing it. Do employees feel overworked? Underpaid? Unappreciated? Are there personality or scheduling problems? Is the work environment itself considered to be positive or negative?

To answer these questions and more, it's necessary to talk to employees and get them to open up to you. You might also want to use a questionnaire similar to the one shown here.

Once you have the questionnaires back, you'll be in a good position to identify any underlying problems that exist and work to reduce or eliminate them. In so doing, you'll be on your way to maintaining high employee morale.

EMPLOYEE SATISFACTION QUESTIONNAIRE

	USUALLY	SOMETIMES	NEVER
1. In achieving the goals of the business I am also able to achieve my own.	_____	_____	_____
2. I feel that I am treated fairly.	_____	_____	_____
3. The standards of performance set for my job are reasonable.	_____	_____	_____
4. My job description accurately describes my duties.	_____	_____	_____
5. I receive timely and objective performance appraisals.	_____	_____	_____
6. I am given sufficient information to do my job.	_____	_____	_____
7. I am encouraged to come up with new ideas.	_____	_____	_____
8. The work I do is challenging.	_____	_____	_____
9. My working conditions are good.	_____	_____	_____
10. I feel adequately paid.	_____	_____	_____
11. The job pressures are manageable.	_____	_____	_____
12. Training is available to me.	_____	_____	_____

	USUALLY	SOMETIMES	NEVER
13. The business promotes qualified employees.			
14. My fringe benefits are comparable with those at other businesses.			
15. I feel appreciated.			
16. I feel secure in my job.			
17. I take pride in the work I do.			
18. I'm kept informed on matters that affect me.			
19. Employee complaints are dealt with quickly and fairly.			
20. I have a say in the decision-making process.			
21. Employees at all levels work as a team.			
22. My contributions are recognized.			
23. Employees generally like it here.			
24. This is a good place to work.			

6 | DELEGATING AUTHORITY

One of the major decision areas confronting each business owner during crucial growth stages is the matter of authority. How much authority should be delegated? To whom? When? How? The way you answer these questions will, to a great extent, determine not only the organizational structure of your business, but what it's able to accomplish.

LETTING GO

The hardest thing for many entrepreneurs to do is to share decision-making power with others. Having personally overseen and often carried out most of the tasks necessary to build their businesses, they're reluctant to delegate authority to anyone else. Call it ego or call it fear, the general attitude is "If you want something done right, do it yourself." Utilizing the same "hands on" method that got their businesses started, these entrepreneurs want to be involved in everything—from the biggest decision to the smallest detail. What they don't realize is that, while this approach was effective—even necessary—in the beginning, it's now holding them back and hurting their businesses.

No matter how talented and energetic you are, the fact remains that *you can't do everything yourself.* And you shouldn't.

When a business owner tries to do it all, what usually happens is:

▶ **The business stays small.** To keep it manageable the owner must limit its size.

▶ **Profitable opportunities are ignored.** Without managers authorized to research and develop new products and services, the business tends to stick with its existing ones.

▶ **Employees are less productive.** Rather than showing initiative and seeking out better ways to accomplish the business's objectives, employees simply do what they are told.

▶ **The best employees leave.** Put off by the owner's refusal to give them more responsibility and authority, the most talented employees go to work for someone else who recognizes and utilizes their abilities. Or they go into business for themselves and often become competitors.

▶ **Long-range planning suffers.** Since the owner is caught up with the day-to-day aspects of running the business there's little time left to focus on where the business is headed and what its objectives are.

▶ **The owner burns out.** The day-after-day shouldering of the entire responsibility for the business's success eventually takes its toll—physically and emotionally.

The entrepreneur's need to directly control every aspect of the business operation keeps the business and everyone associated with it from developing any further. Painful as it may be, "If you want your business to grow, you have to let go."

WHAT CAN BE DELEGATED?

Depending on the nature of your business and your preferences, some areas of operation will call for a higher degree of control than others. In areas where a high degree of control is needed, most of the authority is likely to be retained by you. Conversely, in areas needing only a low degree of control, authority is likely to be delegated to others whenever possible.

One business owner may feel that the area requiring the highest degree of control is money management and make all

DEGREE OF OWNER CONTROL REQUIRED

CONTROL AREA	LOW	MEDIUM	HIGH
Finances			
Production			
Quality assurance			
Customer service			
Distribution			
Sales			
Pricing			
Promotion			
Public relations			
Personnel			
Purchasing			
Inventory control			
Planning			
Research and development			
Security			
Maintenance			
Legal			

or most of the decisions pertaining to the business's finances. Another entrepreneur, say in retailing, might have a different view, focusing on the buying area instead, since it's critical for a store to carry the merchandise that customers want.

Since different businesses have different needs, your first step in the delegation process should be to determine how much control you're willing to relinquish in each area. To help get you started, use the preceding chart to assess the degree of control you need in each of the areas shown.

Once you've determined the areas most in need of your personal attention, you can then formulate a plan for delegating authority where less control is required, freeing yourself to work on those things that are critical to your success.

OWNER'S CIRCLE OF DELEGATION

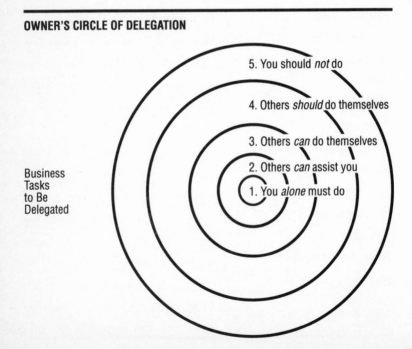

Business
Tasks
to Be
Delegated

5. You should *not* do

4. Others *should* do themselves

3. Others *can* do themselves

2. Others *can* assist you

1. You *alone* must do

As you can see from the Owner's Circle of Delegation, most of your time should be spent on number 1- and number 2-level tasks, while tasks in the circle's outer ring are to be avoided altogether.

Whether a task is a 1 or a 5 depends on the degree of control required, the importance of the task, the personnel, and the time available to carry it out. For example, the decision to relocate your business to another city or to change its name would be either a number 1- or 2-level task depending on how much input you want from others. Choosing a custodial service to provide everyday maintenance, on the other hand, might range from a number 2- to a 4-task, while reordering office supplies is a 5.

THE DELEGATION PROCESS

A frequent mistake made by business owners and managers is to assume that by delegating authority to a subordinate the delegation process is complete. Authority is just one of three elements in the delegation process. The other two—responsibility and accountability—must also be present if you are to get positive results.

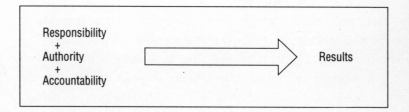

Responsibility

The delegation process starts by assigning specific responsibilities. The employee should be fully informed of what he or she is expected to do when hired, promoted, transferred, or given a new assignment. For all the job functions or activities necessary to fulfill an assignment, *responsibility should generally be delegated to the lowest competent level in your business*. The lower, the better. As long as the person has the knowledge, skills, and willingness it takes to carry out the job.

Authority

In delegating authority to an employee, you are giving him or her the right to make decisions and the power to carry them out. The amount of authority that should be delegated depends on the nature of each employee's job and responsibilities. At a minimum, delegate enough authority (1) to get the work done, (2) to allow key employees to take initiative, and (3) to keep things going in your absence.

Accountability

Accountability refers to the obligation all employees have to fulfill the responsibilities that have been assigned to them. However, unlike the other two elements in the delegation process, accountability cannot be delegated. It is something that an employee chooses to accept or not to accept. If an employee rejects his or her obligation, then you, as the owner, must ultimately be held accountable. This should always be kept in mind. Since, in the end, "the buck stops with you."

In keeping with what management experts call the "parity principle," all three elements of the delegation process should be present in equal amounts. For example, when you assign responsibility for a specific task, the activities to be performed should not exceed the employee's authority to carry them out. Thus, if you give your assistant a major project to complete, such as preparing a video presentation for an upcoming meeting, the assistant must have the authority to obtain the necessary information to be included in the presentation. As for accountability, proper screening and training of employees, along with proper delegation, can help to bring this in balance with the other two elements.

CENTRALIZED VERSUS DECENTRALIZED AUTHORITY

The amount of authority you delegate and how extensively it is spread throughout your business will determine whether the business's organizational structure is *centralized* or *decentralized.* As shown in this chart, if little or no authority is delegated, a business is centralized; the owner, alone, or perhaps with a small group of top managers, makes most of the decisions concerning the business. If, however, authority is widely distributed among employees at all levels in the business, it is decentralized. In this case, employees participate in most of the decision-making.

DISTRIBUTION OF AUTHORITY

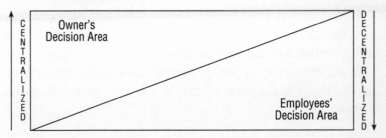

There is something to be said for both approaches to delegation. It isn't so much a question of which is better, but which is better for *you.*

To determine whether a centralized or decentralized organizational structure best suits your business, compare the advantages and disadvantages of each.

CENTRALIZED AUTHORITY

ADVANTAGES	DISADVANTAGES
You can make quick decisions.	More information may be needed to make a decision.
Policies can be uniformly implemented.	Greater demands are placed on you and your top managers.
Activities can be coordinated more easily.	Decisions often reflect a narrow viewpoint.
Accountability can be readily determined.	You receive less feedback from employees.
The level of duplicated effort is reduced.	Employees at lower levels may feel left out.
Less time is spent in meetings.	

Having looked at what each has to offer, you may find that one organizational structure is significantly better than the other, or that a combination of the two is what you need.

In assessing the degree of centralization most appropriate for your business, some of the factors you should consider include:

▶ The costs involved
▶ The impact on your business's policies and practices
▶ The skills and talents of your employees
▶ The willingness of employees to accept accountability
▶ Employees' access to information
▶ The speed with which decisions must be made

DECENTRALIZED AUTHORITY

ADVANTAGES	DISADVANTAGES
You can spend more time focusing on key areas.	More time is spent getting a consensus of opinion.
Employees can deal with problems as they occur.	A greater amount of time and money is spent on training.
Employees gain experience in decision-making.	The consistency and quality of decisions may vary.
Employees are more likely to be strongly motivated.	It can undermine the unity of the business's objectives.
It's easier to expand your business.	Accountability is harder to establish.
The skills and abilities of all employees can be utilized.	

▶ The effect on employee morale
▶ Your own willingness to relinquish control
▶ Your objectives for the business

SPAN OF CONTROL

A separate area of delegation that goes hand in hand with centralization and decentralization is *span of control*—the number of workers who report to each supervisor. If your business is small, it's likely that each worker reports directly to you. If this is the case, your span of control is equal to the number of employees who work for you.

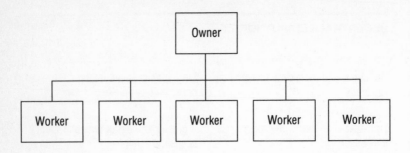

As your business expands, span of control becomes more important. At this stage you must decide what is the ideal number of workers you can supervise. Furthermore, with the addition of each manager to aid in the supervision process, his or her own span of control must also be determined. As shown in the following chart, narrowing your span of control and that of your managers increases the organizational levels needed.

The wider the span of control you use, the more centralized your business will be.

WIDE SPAN OF CONTROL—FOUR PERSONS
4 Managers
2 Levels of Management

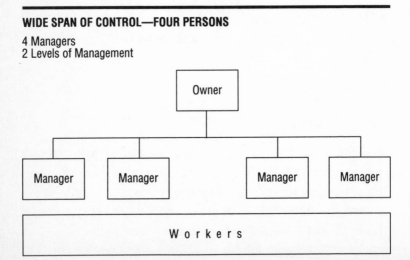

Ultimately, it comes down to a choice between a wide span of control and a few levels (or even one level) of management or a narrow span of control and more levels of management. The wide span gives you and your managers greater control, but it also puts a greater burden of responsibility on you. The narrow span relieves this burden but, by adding extra levels, it is more costly and makes communication more complicated.

Although on the surface it might seem like a simple matter of mathematics, determining the appropriate span of control is more involved than that. In fact, no one span of control works best; each situation and each person is different. One manager may be perfectly at ease supervising fifty or more employees, while another manager is uncomfortable with five. In evaluating

NARROW SPAN OF CONTROL—TWO PERSONS
6 Managers
3 Levels of Management

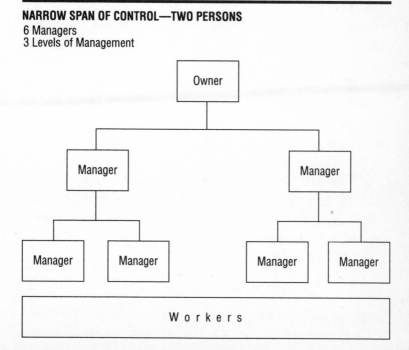

your current situation or anticipating future needs, keep in mind:

1. **Your own skills as a manager.** Many entrepreneurs are excellent at coming up with new ideas but have difficulty implementing them. This may be due to lack of management training, lack of time, or both. Narrowing the span of control can compensate for this, shifting more of the responsibility to others.

2. **The skills of your current managers or those in line for management positions.** The greater their abilities, the wider the span of control that can be used.

3. **The competence of the employees being supervised.** When you can count on employees to work competently and independently there can be a wider span of control.

4. **The activities being performed.** Activities that are basically similar and routine can usually be handled with a wide span of control. Conversely, dissimilar activities normally require a narrow span of control.

5. **The size of your business.** Generally as a business grows—whether in the number of employees, locations, or product lines—the span of control gets narrower. This is particularly true at the owner's level, since it enables the owner to focus on fewer decision areas at a time.

6. **The presence of set policies and procedures.** The extent to which policies and procedures are set in advance also affects the span of control. The more they are predetermined, the wider the span of control possible.

ADAPTING TO CHANGE

Whatever systems of control you use—centralized or decentralized authority, a wide or narrow span of control—there's a good chance you will have to modify them. More and more successful businesses are recognizing the need to develop flexible organizational structures. Rather than developing what seems to be the perfect system of control and then sticking with it no matter what, you must be prepared to adapt to change.

Bottom-Up Organizations

Many management specialists now advocate getting rid of traditional organization charts that show each person's position and authority; or turning them upside down, creating "bottom up" organizations of empowered employees with greater authority—based on the premise that lower-level employees are closer to the customer and therefore should have a greater say in matters affecting the product delivery process (i.e., production, quality control, pricing, promotion, distribution, and so on). Another approach to empowering workers that's been implemented particularly in the manufacturing field is the use of *quality circles;* groups of workers who meet periodically to discuss ways to increase productivity and job satisfaction.

The Virtual Corporation

One of the more innovative developments in ways to organize a business has been the emergence of the *virtual corporation;* a temporary network of independent companies agreeing to work together to capitalize on a specific opportunity. Having applications for both big businesses that want to get things done faster and small businesses that have scant resources, it takes the joint venture form to a higher level in which businesses share only their "core competencies"—the things they do best. For instance, one business might provide the technical know-how to develop a product; a second business, the manufacturing skills to produce it; and a third business, the sales force to sell it.

In addition to providing needed resources that each business is lacking, this method of organization also saves time, enabling various functions to be carried out *concurrently*, rather than sequentially, often by workers (designers, engineers, suppliers, product managers, etc.) linked together via computer. A modern version of the *keiretsu*—the collaborative business combinations long favored by the Japanese—virtual corporations have been utilized by such well-known American companies as Apple and MCI.

In a virtual corporation, delegation of authority not only takes place within each business, but *between* businesses, as each one shares its skills, information, and resources with the others. Representing the nth degree in decentralization, in this type of borderless configuration it's sometimes hard to tell where one business ends and another begins. An entrepreneur who enters into one of these alliances must be willing to relinquish control in those areas outside his or her company's core competencies and to be part of a team.

In determining whether this business structure could work for you, it's important to make sure that the benefits (increased strength and flexibility) offset the liabilities (diluted control, potential loss of proprietary information, and the effort it takes to adapt to the format). Then pick your partners carefully, since you will be depending on them.

7 | MASTERING THE MARKETPLACE

Getting a toehold in the marketplace is hard enough. Keeping it can be even harder. One of the biggest challenges for a growing business is coming up with improved ways to direct the flow of goods and services to its customers. To sustain growth you must not only be able to make a good product, but to market it. This means finding out what customers want *before* you produce it and then doing what's necessary to put it within their reach.

The larger your business grows, the more important it is to have an integrated marketing system that's capable of satisfying customers' needs, identifying new groups to serve, and monitoring changes in the marketplace. Rather than being viewed as a supplemental activity that follows production, marketing must be seen as a core activity that *precedes* production, guiding your planning efforts and affecting all aspects of your business.

To fend off competitors and continue to expand, your business must:

► Recognize customers' needs
► Create products and services to satisfy those needs
► Identify new target markets to serve
► Select the best distribution channels to use
► Develop profitable pricing strategies
► Communicate effectively with potential customers
► Build a positive business image

Being aware of your environment is critical. The first step toward mastering the marketplace, though, isn't to look outside your business; it's to look within, focusing on your strengths and weaknesses and what it is that sets you apart from the competition.

KNOW YOUR USP

When a business grows, one of the things that often gets lost in the process is its identity. Because of the desire to reach more people and to increase market share, the business goes in several directions at once. Instead of doing what it does best, it tries to be all things to all people . . . and ends up being nothing to anyone.

The way to avoid this is to know your USP—your *unique selling proposition*. In essence, this is what makes your business special and gives customers a reason to buy from you. For example, possible USPs include the following:

► High quality
► Superior service
► Innovative ideas
► One-of-a-kind products
► Low prices
► Wide selection
► Reliability

► Fast work
► State-of-the-art technology
► Caring people
► Unconditional guarantees
► Convenience
► Expertise

Defining who and what your business is, your USP should be the underlying concept behind your marketing strategy. In the insurance field, for instance, one has only to think of some of the leading companies' slogans to know their USPs. Prudential's "Get a piece of the rock" puts the emphasis on reliability. State Farm wants you to know it cares, "Just like a good neighbor, State Farm is there." And Allstate offers superior service, as evidenced by the promise "You're in good hands with Allstate."

The stronger your USP, the more effective you'll be at marketing your products and services. Rather than having to guess what your business has to offer, customers will know. To really do the job, though, your USP must be:

- In tune with customers' needs
- Presented in a believable way
- Something people remember
- Able to motivate customers to buy

In tune with customers' needs. Having a USP that matches customers' needs tells customers that if they buy from you they will receive satisfaction. Your business specializes in the very thing that's important to them and can provide what they want better than the competition can.

Presented in a believable way. Saying what you can do is one thing. Making customers believe it is another. How you state your USP and present it in your advertising and other communications will affect how customers react to it. If they think you're lying, customers won't buy. Isuzu recognized the skepticism customers have about automobile manufacturers' claims (especially the car salespeople who make them) and used this to its advantage in its humorous commercials featuring Joe Isuzu, the lying car salesman who would promise anything.

Something people remember. One of the hardest things to do is to articulate your USP in a way that it sticks in customers' minds. With so many messages and slogans fighting for customers' attention, it's difficult to stand out from the crowd. Two companies that managed to do this very effectively using just a single word are 7-Up and Heinz. By coining the word "uncola," 7-Up instantly and memorably told customers that its soft drink was different from the rest. Heinz used the music and the title of the Carly Simon hit song "Anticipation" to demonstrate that its thicker, slower-pouring ketchup was something worth waiting for.

Able to motivate customers to buy. A good USP must be able to sell. Otherwise it's merely descriptive. This is why it's so important to match your strengths to customers' needs. The goal is to make your product or service an indispensable part of customers' lives. Federal Express's claim that it's the one to use when your package "absolutely, positively" has to be there, leaves no room for doubt that businesses that want to *stay* in business call FedEx.

KNOW YOUR TARGET MARKET

In addition to knowing your USP, you must also know your target market. The best USP in the world won't do you much good if your target market has shifted or shrunk, or wasn't there to begin with. Many businesses fail to realize this until they are well into the start-up phase or beyond. Then, all of a sudden, it hits them—"Who are we doing this for?" Having gotten that far, they don't really know who their customers are or what they want.

This comes from having a *production orientation* that concentrates on what the business can produce, rather than a *con-*

MASTERING THE MARKETPLACE 83

sumer orientation that concentrates on the consumer needs that are unfilled. Manufacturing and high-technology businesses are particularly vulnerable to this since they often become enamored with their own capabilities—"We *can* make it; therefore we will." It's a much more common mistake than you might think.

People Over Products

As any designer will tell you, "Form follows function." Something similar can be said for marketing. Only in this case it would be "Products follow people." Rather than trying to create needs for existing products (or services), successful businesses create products for existing needs. This way, the people in your target market determine what you offer and what you don't. For that to happen, though, you must know who your target market is.

Identifying Your Target Market

To find out which people or organizations make up your target market start by:

▶ Seeking out consumers whose needs are not currently being satisfied.
▶ Matching marketing opportunities to your business's resources and objectives.
▶ Focusing on those groups, or *market segments*, you can most profitably serve.
▶ Choosing one or more segments (target markets) whose needs you wish to fill.

As shown in this chart, there are a number of *consumer variables* you can use to divide the total market into individual market segments.

SEGMENTATION VARIABLES—CONSUMER MARKETS

DEMOGRAPHIC VARIABLES

Age
Sex
Marital status
Family size
Family life cycle
Income
Occupation
Education
Race
Ethnic background
Religion

PSYCHOGRAPHIC VARIABLES

Personality type
Values
Beliefs
Activities
Interests/hobbies
Opinions—liberal/conservative
Self-image
Concerns
Motives
Attitudes

GEOGRAPHIC VARIABLES

International
National
Regional
Urban, suburban, rural
Market size
Climate
Terrain

BEHAVIORISTIC VARIABLES

Benefits expected
Usage level
Brand loyalty
Purchase occasion
Shopping situation

These variables can be used separately or in combination with each other. Which ones you choose will depend on the resources and objectives of your business and the kinds of needs you are prepared to fill.

Demographic segmentation. Segmenting the market according to demographic variables uses population statistics such as age, sex, and income to construct potential target markets. For instance, a cosmetics manufacturer might target teen-aged girls. Or a travel agency could direct its efforts toward middle-aged couples whose children are no longer at home—"empty nesters" with the time and money to travel. One restaurant might cater to the needs of families, providing food at affordable prices with special meals for children, while another restaurant focuses its attention on affluent adults seeking a gourmet dining experience in a romantic setting.

Psychographic segmentation. Psychographic variables based on consumers' personalities and lifestyles can also be used to segment the market. Since much of the data pertains to consumers' activities, interests, and opinions, it's sometimes called *AIO data*. Although more difficult to obtain than demographic data, it can be extremely useful in identifying consumer needs and wants. For example, a luxury sedan and a high-powered sports car may cost the same, but they appeal to a different type of person. The person who buys the sedan is more likely to be a low-key, conservative type who values conformity and comfort. The person who opts for the sports car, on the other hand, is more likely to be outgoing and independent, placing a higher value on mechanical performance than comfort.

Geographic segmentation. Where people live has a much greater impact on what they buy than businesses sometimes realize. This is particularly true for businesses engaged in international marketing; but even within the United States itself, consumer tastes, preferences, and needs vary from one part of the country to another. Everything from the foods they eat and the clothes they wear to the cars they drive and the homes they live in are affected; in rugged terrain, four-wheel drive vehicles may be a necessity, not a choice, and in cold climates, clothing is likely to be chosen as much for warmth as fashion. Consumers who live in coastal areas can be expected to eat more seafood, while those in the sunbelt states generally eat more fresh produce.

Behavioristic segmentation. Focusing on how and when purchases are made, behavioristic variables divide the market into "users" and "nonusers," classifying the users as being "light," "moderate," or "heavy." *Heavy users* are a particularly desirable segment since they often account for the bulk of a product's sales. Marketers refer to this phenomenon as the *80/20 rule*, which states that "80 percent of a product's sales are likely to come from just 20 percent of its customers." Other variables such as brand loyalty and the kinds of benefits expected (i.e., convenience, safety, durability, and so on), are also important. So are the circumstances of the purchase. Is the product something people buy for themselves or as a gift? Will they buy it on impulse or after careful deliberation?

Just as the market can be divided into different consumer segments, it can also be divided into *organizational segments* focusing on the needs of businesses and other organizations. Some of the most commonly used segmentation variables are shown here:

SEGMENTATION VARIABLES—ORGANIZATIONAL MARKETS

—Profit or Nonprofit	—Location
—Type of organization	—Size
Manufacturing	—Number of employees
Wholesale	—Annual revenues
Retail	—Budget considerations
Service	—Corporate culture
—Industry/field	—Policies & procedures

Selecting the right segmentation variables can make all the difference in correctly identifying your target market. Rather than wasting your time trying to sell to or service the wrong groups, you can zero in on the ones most likely to be your customers.

FINE TUNE YOUR MARKETING MIX

The more you know about your target market, the greater your ability to create the best *marketing mix.* Also called the "4 Ps," this consists of the four components—*product* (or service), *price, promotion,* and *place*—you put together to satisfy prospective customers. The key ingredients in your product offering, these components are the only things in the marketplace that you control, and the decisions that you make regarding each one will determine how successful your business ultimately becomes.

MARKETING MIX DECISION AREAS

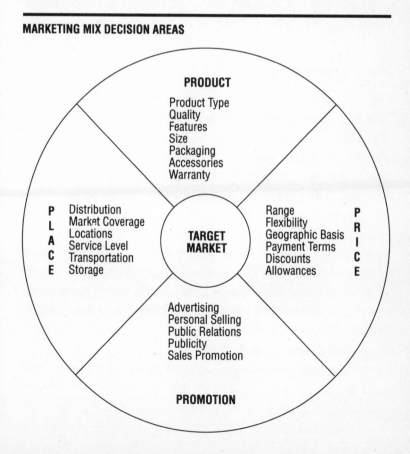

PRODUCT

Product Type
Quality
Features
Size
Packaging
Accessories
Warranty

PLACE

Distribution
Market Coverage
Locations
Service Level
Transportation
Storage

TARGET MARKET

PRICE

Range
Flexibility
Geographic Basis
Payment Terms
Discounts
Allowances

Advertising
Personal Selling
Public Relations
Publicity
Sales Promotion

PROMOTION

No matter how good your marketing mix is, you must continue to adjust it as your business grows or moves from one stage to another. It's imperative that you keep looking for ways to improve your production and distribution techniques, to price more profitably, and to strengthen your bonds with customers.

In fine-tuning your marketing mix, keep in mind that changing one component often means changing other components, as well. For example, if you add more product features, it may force you to raise prices. Switching from one distribution channel to another is likely to affect your promotion strategy, too.

As you can see from the marketing mix components shown, there are a number of decision areas in each component.

Product Decisions

Deciding what type of product or service to offer is just the first of many product-related decisions an entrepreneur makes. Regardless of what field you're in, you must continue to evaluate and reevaluate your product and its associated benefits. A greeting card manufacturer, for instance, must decide on the look and feel of the cards. Should they be printed on expensive parchment or on recycled paper? Have humorous or serious messages? Utilize a particular theme or character? Be sold singly or by the box? Along with this, the card manufacturer must determine when it's time to add new cards to the line or to drop old ones. And suppose a character featured in the cards develops a following with consumers. Would it be a good idea to create a line of novelty items, too, such as dolls, T-shirts, mugs, and desk accessories?

To keep your products and services fresh and appealing, you can't let up on your efforts to find better ways to design, package, and present them. Whether you're debating the merits of restyling your product, making it available in different sizes, or extending its warranty, there are countless decisions to be made.

Price Decisions

The second most important marketing mix decision—after the product type itself—is what price to charge. Price, more than any other factor, is the determinant that convinces people to buy. Telling customers more than just the affordability of a product, the price tells them what to expect in the way of value, quality, prestige, and practicality. Setting the right price is critical. A price that's too low will cause customers to question the quality of the product or service and wonder if it's somehow inferior. A price that's too high will make customers think you're taking advantage of them.

To determine price range, there are several strategies that you can use based on your overall marketing mix objectives. These are some of the more common ones:

Penetration pricing. Businesses that use this strategy set their prices low and keep them low in order to penetrate the marketplace and reach as many customers as possible. To be effective it calls for low profit margins and high sales volumes. If you select this option, you'll need to keep your product costs down and achieve wide market coverage.

Skimming. This pricing strategy entails setting a high initial price for your product and then lowering it over time as the product gains in customer acceptance. A popular strategy in the computer and electronics fields, it offers the advantage of enabling companies to recoup their research and development costs more quickly. For it to work, you'll need to have a superior product that can be promoted and distributed to a narrow target market of "innovators" willing to pay more for the latest products.

Prestige pricing. As the name implies, this pricing strategy uses high prices to create a prestigious product image. To avoid having it backfire on you, though, it's essential to have a high-quality product and to provide the personalized service and selling that customers would expect to receive.

Finding the right price range for your product or service is just the beginning. Other pricing decisions that you need to consider as your business grows center on such things as price flexibility (having fixed prices versus negotiated ones), the type of discounts to offer, payment terms, and so on.

Promotion Decisions

Promotion encompasses all of the activities that enable businesses to communicate with their potential customers and the general public. One of the key decisions you must make here is whether to rely more on personal selling or advertising to reach your target market. Personal selling has the advantage of providing one-on-one attention, but it's less effective (and more expensive) for reaching a mass market. Advertising via the media—newspapers, magazines, radio, television, and so on—is good at this, but doesn't provide personal interaction or immediate feedback.

The types of products or services you offer will determine, in part, which techniques you use; but so will such factors as your growth rate, distribution methods, budget, and objectives. To achieve your communication goals, you must continue to assess and revise your promotion strategy, varying your methods to match the changing needs of your business and your target market.

To keep your blend of personal selling and advertising in balance with the rest of your marketing mix, use this chart to determine which method works best based on the factors shown.

MARKETING MIX FACTORS/PROMOTION METHODS

FACTORS	PERSONAL SELLING	ADVERTISING
—Product characteristics	High-tech Complex Luxury Unique New	Low-tech Simple Basic Standardized Established
—Price characteristics	High price Negotiated Special terms	Low price Fixed Standard terms
—Place characteristics	Limited distribution High service level	Wide distribution Low service level

Place Decisions

Focusing primarily on where and how your product is sold, place decisions play a pivotal role in growing a business, since they determine whether or not customers have access to your product. In order to master the marketplace, you must *be* in the marketplace. This entails choosing which distribution channels work best, finding the right outlets to use, and keeping inventory, storage, and transportation costs down.

Much of your success at achieving your goals will depend on your ability to build strong relationships with your suppliers and distributors. At all times you must take steps to strengthen your existing alliances and to develop new ones, continually looking for better ways to put your products into customers' hands.

In making your place decisions it's important to consider these factors:

Customers' preferences. Customers' shopping habits and preferred ways of making purchases must be your first consideration. Are they more likely to shop in specialty stores or discount outlets? What type of service level do they expect? How far will they go to obtain your product? How long will they take to find it? Do they prefer to shop by phone or by mail? Or to place orders through their computers?

Business resources/objectives. You must also consider your own needs and preferences. Do you have the necessary resources to distribute the product yourself? Is this something you want to do or would you rather have intermediaries do it? What sales volumes are you seeking? How fast do you want to grow? How important is control? What image do you want to maintain?

Competitors' actions. What distribution methods are your competitors using to reach customers? The more accessible their products or services are, the more accessible yours must be. If your competitors are moving into shopping malls, putting their products into vending machines, or selling them through television shopping networks, these are avenues that you must consider, too. Take automated teller machines, for instance. When banks first started installing them, they were a high-tech novelty. Now, no bank would be without one. Customers not only expect to have instant access to their money, they *demand* it.

Product requirements. The needs of the product itself can't be overlooked. What kind of attention and handling does it require? Is it perishable or durable? Expensive or inexpensive? Does it need to be demonstrated or can customers just buy it off the shelf?

WATCH YOUR ENVIRONMENT

You can control your marketing mix. But you can't control your environment. The marketplace is constantly changing and in order to make the right marketing decisions you must pay close attention to the changes taking place in these sectors:

- Economics
- Society
- Competition
- Technology
- Politics

Economics

Inflation, interest rates, taxes, unemployment, and other economic factors have a direct influence on consumers' spending habits and willingness to buy various products and services. When the economy is strong and job prospects are good, people are more willing to buy luxury items and to spend more for higher quality. During a recession the opposite is true as people economize and place a high priority on "value"—getting the most for their money.

Society

Shifts in population, age, income, family size, and living arrangements must also be closely monitored, along with changes in culture and social behavior. For instance, as the 76 million "baby boomers" born between 1946 and 1964 continue to move from one life stage to the next, getting married, raising families, retiring, the demand changes from one product to another—

sports cars give way to minivans, dinner and a movie to home-delivered pizza and a video. Increases in the number of working women, singles, couples without children ("DINKs"—dual income, no kids), and ethnic minorities are also changing the way America shops.

Competition
The competitive landscape is subject to change at a moment's notice as new types of businesses enter the marketplace and others leave. The store across the street may be the least of your problems. The real competitive threat may come from the catalogue waiting in customers' mail boxes or the 24-hour television shopping network that's just a remote control and a phone call away. Staying competitive means staying informed about competitors' actions and being ready to make changes in your marketing mix as needed.

Technology
Technology, like time, waits for no man. To keep your business or products from becoming obsolete, it's essential for you to be aware of the latest developments in your field. The more quickly you can spot new technologies and put them to work, saving time or money, improving your product, or speeding delivery, the better your product offering will be.

Politics
Changes in the political/legal environment can also have a strong effect on the demand for products. Laws, regulations, and taxes contribute to a product's availability and cost, making it more desirable or less so. Correctly interpreting the impact that a proposed law or new requirement will have on your business can enable you to act promptly, doing what's necessary to increase your sales or reduce your losses.

8 | RECOGNIZING OPPORTUNITIES

The more successful a business becomes, the more tempting it is to keep things the way they are, staying with the same products or services, rather than developing new ones. After all, with so much at stake, why take chances? "If it ain't broke, don't fix it." However, playing it safe often proves a more dangerous strategy than venturing into the unknown. To maintain a competitive edge, you must constantly be on the lookout for those new ideas or better ways of doing things that can improve your business or even revolutionize your industry.

RESEARCHING THE MARKET

The three most important things in developing profitable business opportunities are: research, research, and research. The more you know about your environment, the better.

To ensure that your business is fully utilizing its resources and not missing out on desirable opportunities, look to the *past* and the *future*. First, look to the past to determine your business's strengths and weaknesses, then try to predict which trends or changes in consumer demand you can capitalize on. By taking the time to research the market in this way, you may discover that a previously strong product or service is becoming obsolete because of technological advances or changes in customer needs. On the other hand, a little-noticed product or service may actually be growing in popularity, possibly for the very same reasons. For example, sales of computer workstations may be dropping off while sales of laptops are increasing.

Sources of Marketing Information

One of the greatest needs of business owners today is for accurate and current information on which to base their marketing decisions. Who are your customers? Where are they? Why do they buy? How often do they buy? How much do they spend? What sizes, colors, shapes, styles, or flavors do they prefer? Is the demand for your products or services rising or falling? Who is your competition? What effect does the economy have on your business? What new customers or markets can you reach? Knowing the answers to these questions and more is the key to capitalizing on new opportunities.

Although researching the market may sound difficult, costly, and time-consuming, it's a lot easier than it seems. What's more, most of the information you need is already in your possession or can be readily acquired. Some of your best sources of marketing information include: your business records, customers, salespeople, suppliers, trade associations, government, and the media.

Business Records
In addition to monitoring your business's income statement and balance sheet figures, also keep close tabs on your sales

records, noting the revenues and expenses by product, product line, type of service, sales territory (or store), and so on. This not only enables you to determine what your sales level is, but also *why*. Do some products move faster than others? Which products aren't moving at all? Are certain colors or styles more in demand now than they were last year? Are selling costs for a particular product or service rising faster than the corresponding profits?

Customers

Paying attention to customers' shopping habits and buying patterns is another way to gather marketing information. This can be accomplished by observation, surveys, or questionnaires. Or you can conduct *focus group sessions* in which customers (usually from five to fifteen) talk about their individual needs and attitudes relative to your products or services. Focus group sessions can be particularly useful in providing feedback about the image of your business, the competence and friendliness of personnel, the way you compare with the competition, shifts in consumer needs, and more.

Salespeople

Your own salespeople are especially good sources of marketing information. They, more than anyone else, come into direct contact with customers on a regular basis. This puts them in an ideal position to discover which customer needs are being overlooked and what new trends are developing, as well as to detect changes in competitors' sales strategies. To make sure that this information isn't wasted, it helps to institute a reporting system that provides you with ready access to salespeople's findings.

Suppliers

Don't hesitate to ask your suppliers what's happening in the marketplace. A good supplier should do more than just fill orders on time. Part of a supplier's job is to keep an eye on the developments in his or her industry and to help business owners make the right purchasing decisions. This means knowing the details of a competitor's upcoming advertising campaign; the current research in your field; what new products are about to be launched; proposed price increases, and so on.

Trade Associations

Trade associations can provide you with marketing information in a variety of areas related to your business. This includes forecasts of future demand levels and trends; cost studies; statistics on your industry's policies, practices, and pay scales; the impact of proposed changes in government regulations. As a member of the business community, it's to your advantage to find out about the trade associations that represent your industry and then make a point to get in touch with them.

Government

Government agencies at the federal, state, and local levels can supply you with a wealth of marketing research data at little or no cost. The Department of Commerce, Economic Development Offices, and the Small Business Administration are just a few of the agencies you can contact for information. In addition to having specialists on staff to answer your questions, these agencies produce reports on all aspects of the economy, including changes in the population (age, income, education, family status, and other demographic data), sales trends, construction activity, and other areas. Many of these reports are available at your local library. For more information on the help available from the government, see Chapter Fourteen.

The Media

To spot the trends of tomorrow, it's important to be tuned into today. Entrepreneurs often become so involved in their business operations that they block out the world around them and fail to notice events that may have an impact on their businesses. No matter how busy your schedule is, each week set aside a certain amount of time to catch up on current events. By plugging into the media, you may find that the information in a newspaper or magazine article or radio or television program can help to resolve a current problem or point your business in a new direction.

THE PRODUCT LIFE CYCLE

To anticipate changes in the demand for your products or services or to evaluate the demand for new ones, you need to determine their positions within the *product life cycle*. Marketing researchers generally agree that all products and services evolve through a series of stages during which the demand for them peaks and then eventually falls. As shown in the chart on page 100, the product life cycle has *four stages*.

Introduction

In the *introductory stage* the product (or service) isn't yet known to the general public. Whether the product has been newly invented (a solar-powered automobile) or is simply "new and improved" (a stronger soap detergent), it is seeking to become recognized. The marketing goal at this time is to educate potential customers about the benefits to be gained from using the product and to create an increasing demand for it.

Growth

In the *growth stage* a product is beginning to establish a name

PRODUCT LIFE CYCLE

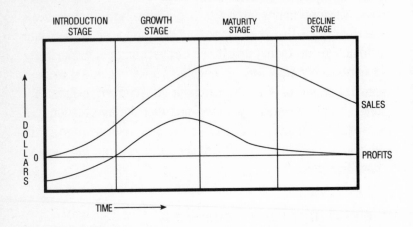

for itself. At this time both its sales volume and its profits should be growing at an accelerated rate as customers continue to discover and buy the product. Unfortunately, this same success soon attracts competitors. Unlike in the first stage, the question here isn't "What does the product do?" but "Which brand is best?"

Maturity
In the *maturity stage* a product is well known by the public and may even be a leader in its field. However, given the heavy competition from similar products, its sales growth is already in the process of leveling off or starting to decline. In an effort to boost sales, promotion costs (advertising, cents-off coupons, special offers, and so on) are often increased during this stage. These have the desired effect of prolonging the product's life span but they also cut into its profits.

Decline

In the *decline stage* a product is nearing the end of its life cycle. Made obsolete by newer products, changes in customer preferences, or a saturated market, the product is no longer needed. At this stage profits may become virtually nonexistent as prices are slashed to increase the product's sales volume. But, barring change in the product itself or in the market, this only serves to postpone the inevitable—replacing the old product with a more profitable one.

Although all products go through the product life cycle, the length of time spent in any one stage, or from the beginning to the end of the cycle, varies for each product. A *fad* item, such as a new kitchen gadget, might have a life span of less than a year, whereas today, a refrigerator still has an indefinite life span, at least until a better way of preserving food comes along. Savvy marketers have also discovered that by modifying a product or changing its image they can stretch the product's life cycle; in effect, create a new and improved product. When this happens the product goes back to the beginning of the cycle and starts again. Thus, it's a standard practice in many fields to avoid the decline stage, if at all possible, by continually updating the various products available.

Considering the workings of the product life cycle, you can determine whether a specific product needs to be *promoted, modified,* or *discontinued.* These considerations can also guide you in making the decision whether to add other products or services to those you already offer. The owner of a sporting goods store, for instance, may decide to increase the store's inventory of golf products that are thought to be in the growth stage. At the same time, merchandise for another sport, such as running, which has moved into the maturity or decline stage, might be reduced or eliminated.

GENERATING NEW PRODUCT IDEAS

Because even the best products and services can't stay in demand forever, the continued success of any business depends on its strength in developing new products. The more new product ideas you can generate, the better chance you have of coming up with a money-making product.

While your business is small, most of the responsibility for coming up with ideas will probably rest with you or a few key people. Over time, though, as your business grows, it's advisable to get others involved, too. This gives you more input and makes it easier to get employees behind the new products when they come out.

At this point you may be thinking, "That's fine, but where are these ideas supposed to come from?" Sometimes you get lucky and an idea just occurs out of the blue—the proverbial "whack on the side of the head." Wow! What a great idea. The Slinky was "invented" this way when a spring fell off a workbench . . . and kept on tumbling, planting the seed for the hugely successful toy. More often than not, though, you're going to have to work for your ideas. It was Thomas Edison who said that invention is "one percent inspiration, 99 percent perspiration."

One of the things you can do to get your creative juices flowing is to use *brainstorming* techniques: a systematic approach to generating ideas that lets you channel team members' energies into the product-development process.

Brainstorming

Brainstorming consists of putting together a group of five to fifteen people in a room and conducting a freewheeling discussion of new ways to meet customers' needs. Participants are encouraged to let their imagination run free. The initial focus should be on the *quantity* of ideas generated, not the practicality. In fact, the wilder and wackier the ideas, the better. That gets people thinking in new directions and considering new possibilities.

A brainstorming session is used to create an environment of "controlled chaos" where unforseen "accidents," such as the spring falling on the floor and giving birth to the Slinky, can occur. It's hoped that as ideas flash around the room, sometimes colliding with each other, something will emerge and take hold, suggesting a new product or service you can offer to customers.

Unstructured as it may sound, brainstorming is more than just a bunch of people shouting out ideas. To achieve the desired results, there are some guidelines that must be in place. These include the following:

Brainstorming Guidelines

1. *There must be a group leader.* Someone with good communication skills and a sense of humor is essential. This person's role is to keep the discussion going and to make sure that every idea gets a chance to be heard.

2. *No criticism is allowed.* The purpose of brainstorming is to generate ideas, not to kill them. There will be time enough later to poke holes in the ideas and throw out those that aren't workable. In the beginning it's important for every idea to be given its due.

3. *All participants are equals.* Rank may have its privileges, but not in brainstorming. Everyone from the mail-room clerk to the chief executive officer must have equal status when it comes to contributing ideas. This is the place for first names only; no titles.

4. *Participants should be chosen carefully.* Diversity is the

secret ingredient that makes brainstorming sizzle. In assembling your group, look for people with different backgrounds, perspectives, and personalities. If everyone has the same viewpoint and style, you're not likely to stumble onto those "breakthrough" opportunities that come from looking at things in a new light.

5. *Write down every idea.* To make sure that no idea gets lost in the shuffle, it's important to write them down—where everyone can *see* them. This provides a point of reference and makes it easier to expand on ideas or spin off new ones.

6. *Start out with a warm-up session.* This can be a simple exercise, game, or puzzle that the group is asked to solve. The purpose is to get the ball rolling and put people in a relaxed frame of mind.

7. *Put the outside world on hold.* Nothing interrupts the creative process more than the sound of a ringing phone. To fan the creative spark into a flame, outside interruptions must be kept to a minimum. One way to do this is to hold the brainstorming sessions away from your business—at a hotel, conference center, or other location.

Once your group has generated as many ideas as it can, you're ready to roll up your sleeves and dig for gold; searching out the idea or combination of ideas that can result in a successful product. Having broadened your creative horizons, now you must narrow them, directing your attention to the ideas that hold forth the most promise.

EVALUATING NEW PRODUCTS

To determine whether an idea for a new product or service has marketing potential, use the following New Product Evaluation Chart to rate its suitability for your business. The more checks you put in the "Strong" column, the greater the likelihood that the proposed product will be successful. Conversely, checks in the "Weak" column represent product deficiencies that could limit your ability to develop and market the product successfully.

NEW PRODUCT EVALUATION CHART

PRODUCT CHARACTERISTICS	STRONG	MODERATE	WEAK
1. Compatibility with existing products	_____	_____	_____
2. Compatibility with the business's image	_____	_____	_____
3. Ability to be financed	_____	_____	_____
4. Profit potential	_____	_____	_____
5. Competitive strength	_____	_____	_____
6. Life expectancy	_____	_____	_____
7. Promotability	_____	_____	_____
8. Patent protection	_____	_____	_____
9. Compliance with legal requirements	_____	_____	_____
10. Product safety	_____	_____	_____

In evaluating new product opportunities, keep in mind that a product has to be more than good. It has to be good for *your* business. A product that's right for another business may not be right for yours. The challenge is to find the right "fit"—a product that can be made with your available resources, satisfy customers' needs, and strengthen your business's ability to achieve its objectives.

The road from new product idea to commercialized product can be long and expensive at times, requiring all of your ingenuity and enthusiasm to reach the end. Procter & Gamble spent close to a decade getting Pampers disposable diapers into the marketplace. The longer it takes, the more time and money you will have committed to the project. So it's vital that you establish your evaluation criteria at the outset and do some serious number crunching to determine the profit potential of each proposed product.

GOLDMINE OPPORTUNITIES

Development of new products is critical for long-term success. In focusing on the need to create *new* products, though, businesses often fail to see goldmine opportunities that already exist. Additional sources of revenue that frequently go unnoticed include these moneymakers:

Spin-offs

These are variations or extensions of your original products. Consisting of new sizes, shapes, colors, flavors, styles, qualities, and so on, spin-offs can become more popular (and profitable) than the products or services that launch them. For example, when microwave ovens began to decline because the market for them had become saturated, manufacturers spun off smaller, "half-pint" versions that could go in a den, college dormitory, boat, or recreational vehicle. The units, which were just the thing for heating up a snack or making popcorn, were an instant success.

Throwaways

In your search for new opportunities, ask yourself, "Can any apparently useless by-product or throwaways be sold instead of scrapped?" Castoffs can be turned into treasures at times if a person is alert enough to recognize their value. For instance, more and more golf courses are finding an unexpected source of revenue in their water hazards by retrieving and selling the golf balls submerged in them. Blemished fruits and vegetables, though unsalable to grocery stores, can still be sold to food-processing companies. Metal, glass, plastic, and paper by-products can generally be put to alternative uses or sold to recyclers. Perhaps the most valuable throwaway of all, though, is information—knowledge gained in the course of operating your business that other businesses or individuals would pay dearly to acquire.

Rediscoveries

Sometimes the next best thing to a new discovery is a *re*discovery—a once-popular product that has disappeared from the marketplace, but is once again right for the times. This can be a former product of your own business or another's. Rediscoveries are particularly prevalent in the fashion industry where anything old enough becomes new again. Witness the '90s revival of bellbottom pants and platform shoes—two fashion staples of the '60s. You can find profitable rediscoveries in virtually any field, from toothpaste to candy to motion pictures, as evidenced by the reemergence of Ipana brand toothpaste, Pop Rocks candy, and the box office hit, *The Fugitive*.

Recoveries

These are aging products that have been given new life by finding alternative uses for them. Probably the best known example of a recovery is Arm & Hammer baking soda, a product that had been steadily declining because of the decrease in home baking. By identifying other uses for it—refrigerator deodorizer, carpet freshener, toothpaste, beauty bath, all-purpose cleanser, and more—the company was able to "reposition" the product in consumers' minds, convincing buyers that baking soda wasn't just for baking anymore.

Hybrids

Many new product breakthroughs aren't breakthroughs at all, but simply hybrids—combinations of existing products. Often lackluster or even outright failures individually, in combination, they're suddenly a success. Catalogue retailing giant L. L. Bean's first product, waterproof boots for hunters and fishermen, was a hybrid the company founder made himself, stitching together the leather tops from a pair of hiking boots with the rubber bottoms from a pair of waders.

Transplants

Rather than developing new products from scratch, an increasing number of businesses are transplanting them from overseas. This not only saves time and money, but reduces the risk. Having already proven itself in the foreign market, the transplant is a known quantity with an established track record. This approach worked well for Kellogg. Looking for something new to entice breakfast eaters, it transplanted a European favorite—a mixture of grains, nuts, and fruits that originated in Switzerland—and turned it into its highly successful Mueslix brand cereal.

Whether your ideas are homegrown or come from foreign soil, the important thing is to *have* ideas and be receptive to them. There are profitable opportunities all around you. But you have to know what to look for and how to recognize them.

To keep opportunities from slipping by, your best line of defense is to:

▶ *Nurture a sense of curiosity.* The germ of many great ideas began with the phrase "What if . . . ?"
▶ *Ask questions.* Rather than telling people what you know, find out what *they* know.
▶ *Vary your daily routine.* This will help you to see things with a fresh eye.
▶ *Allow yourself to dream.* Today's flight of fancy can be tomorrow's patent pending.
▶ *Avoid negative people.* They never have new ideas of their own, but will always find flaws in yours.

The main thing to do is to keep an open mind. Then, when opportunity knocks, you're more likely to hear it.

9 | MAINTAINING GOOD CUSTOMER RELATIONS

Growing a business isn't just about making sales. It's about satisfying customers and building long-term relationships that *keep* them buying from you. Over and over. More often than not, the difference between a successful business and one that's just getting by is the successful business's ability to generate repeat sales. Rather than focusing on ringing up the register or writing up the order, the successful business focuses on the customer, identifying other needs that exist and the additional sales to be made by filling them.

Repeat sales not only mean more profits for you, but bigger profit margins. Devising effective promotions, making contact with potential customers, and convincing them to buy takes time and money. According to the United States Office of Consumer Affairs, it costs five times as much to attract new customers as it does to hold onto your current ones. What's more, repeat customers are generally more willing to pay a premium for the satisfaction they receive. So, once you've won them over, keeping customers sold on you is the most cost-effective move you can make; the bottom line is that investing in maintaining good customer relations pays off.

BUILDING A CUSTOMER FRANCHISE

Your ultimate goal should be to develop a loyal following of repeat customers with an expressed preference for your product offering. When this happens you'll have what marketers call a "customer franchise"—a core group of consumers providing a ready market for your goods and services. The lifeblood of a successful business, these are the people who will buy from you year after year, one generation to the next, asking families and friends to do the same.

A customer franchise is a tremendous business asset not only because it represents a pre-sold market for what you have to offer, but for the positive *word-of-mouth publicity* it spreads. As each satisfied customer recommends your business to someone else, the size of your customer base gets bigger and bigger, growing at an exponential rate. As you can see here, if each of ten satisfied customers recommends your business to two people, who then tell two more, and so on . . .

$$
\begin{array}{r}
10 \text{ satisfied customers} \\
\underline{\times\ 2} \text{ others} \\
20 \text{ potential customers} \\
\underline{\times\ 2} \text{ others} \\
40 \text{ potential customers} \\
\underline{\times\ 2} \text{ others} \\
80 \text{ potential customers} \\
10 + 20 + 40 + 80 = 150 \text{ potential customers}
\end{array}
$$

The initial ten customers will have ballooned into a potential market *fifteen times* that size—and will get larger all the time—

all because of your efforts to build your customer franchise and to nurture the relationship you have with each person who buys from you.

PUTTING CUSTOMERS FIRST

Given the importance of having a strong customer franchise, you should put as much work into building yours as you put into your business itself. Regardless of how good your product is or how vast your resources, these won't be enough to guarantee success if you lose sight of your customers. As your business grows you must meet the challenge to keep developing policies and procedures that put the customer first.

One way to do this is to *make customer service not just a department, but a company-wide activity* with everyone, from the top down, committed to satisfying the customer. This approach puts the responsibility for responding to customers' needs on everyone's shoulders. Rather than relegating it to the Customer Service Department (better known as the "Complaint Department"), responsibility is placed in the hands of the people who can most readily satisfy the customer. Examples of this include:

▶ Authorizing salespeople to make merchandise exchanges without having to get a manager's approval.
▶ Letting salespeople follow customers to other departments to assist with purchases.
▶ Enabling office workers to access customer files without going through lengthy channels.
▶ Allowing shipping personnel to use alternate delivery methods when customer emergencies come up.
▶ Authorizing billing department clerks to modify customers' payment schedules within pre-approved guidelines.

Empowering workers in this way will help build morale and spur efficiency by making them feel that they *can* do something to help. Rather than being part of the problem, they are part of the solution. Customers, in turn, will feel that their needs are being attended to—now. Rather than spinning their wheels or getting passed from department to department, they're getting the situation taken care of, putting them in a positive frame of mind about your business and about buying more from you. A win-win situation for everyone.

Ultimately, it means knowing your customers and being able to determine what's important to them so that you can provide the services they need. Not phony services just to charge more fees, but services designed specifically with them in mind.

SERVICE THAT SELLS

One of the best ways to enhance your customer relations and gain a competitive edge is to make service part of your marketing strategy. Instead of thinking of it as a "frill" or something only the most upscale businesses need to provide, service should be thought of as an integral part of any product offering. Both as a sales tool and a basic customer right.

For instance, customers hurrying into a fast-food restaurant to grab a quick bite for lunch don't expect to be seated by a maitre d' or to find linen tablecloths on the tables. But they *do* expect a clean table. And a lot more. They expect to be treated with courtesy and efficiency, to have their orders taken correctly and the food done properly (something Burger King recognized and incorporated into its long-running "Have it your way" commercials). Condiments, napkins, and tableware should be readily accessible, temperature and music levels set for optimum comfort, and restrooms kept spanking clean. A restau-

rant that does any less, no matter how low its prices, can't hope
to keep customers coming back for more.

The question to ask isn't "How little can we do for customers?" but "How much?" An example of this is the increasing
number of restaurants that now let customers fax their orders
ahead of time so that the food is ready when they arrive—
beefing up customer service *and* sales.

Expectations and Satisfaction

Service at its most basic is simply making it easy and enjoyable
to buy from you. The measure of whether your service is
"good" is the degree to which it satisfies your customers (i.e.,
they feel that they got their money's worth). This, in turn,
depends on what they *expected* to get. Buying a dozen dough-
nuts and getting thirteeen—a "baker's dozen"—is a pleasant
(and satisfying) surprise. On the other hand, a customer who
purchases a supposedly "user-friendly" computer program that
comes with an indecipherable instruction manual is bound to be
disappointed. In the first instance, the customer got more than
was expected; in the second, the customer got less. Thus, the
key to offering service that satisfies is understanding and
managing customers' expectations. As shown in this formula,
there are two main components of customer satisfaction:

$$\text{Customer Satisfaction} = \frac{\text{Delivered Performance}}{\text{Expected Performance}}$$

"Expected performance" is what customers *think* they are
getting when they buy a product or service. "Delivered performance" is what customers *actually* get. The more customers

expect, the better the delivered performance must be to make them satisfied.

Given the relationship between the two kinds of performance—the one expected and the one delivered—you can increase customer satisfaction by either (1) lowering customers' expectations or (2) raising your delivery capabilities. Or, better yet, do both. In the words of customer service professionals: "Promise less, deliver more."

Some of the ways you can keep customers' expectations in balance with your delivered performance include:

▶ **Making realistic projections**—detailing costs, delivery dates, installation times, etc., so that there aren't any unpleasant surprises later on.

▶ **Being specific**—explaining what the product will or will not do, what's standard and what's extra.

▶ **Keeping jargon to a minimum**—using terms that customers can readily understand.

▶ **Avoiding hype**—sidestepping claims like "This skin cream will make you look like a teenager again" and "After a few lessons you'll be playing golf like Jack Nicklaus," which creates false hopes you can't possibly live up to.

▶ **Being honest**—telling customers the truth about what they're buying . . . even if it means losing the sale.

▶ **Keeping customers informed**—letting them know if there's a problem or a delay of some sort and telling them what you're doing to remedy it.

▶ **Going the extra mile**—doing whatever you can to ensure that customers get the best service possible.

By following these guidelines you should not only be able to meet customers' expectations, but to *exceed* them.

STAYING IN TOUCH

As a business grows, it's easy to become distanced from customers and lose track of who they are and what they do. What were their needs when they first started buying from you? What are their needs now? The teenage computer whiz is now a college graduate working as a systems analyst. The little business you gave credit to when no one else would is now one of your biggest accounts. Where did the time go? If you don't stay in touch, you'll be asking a different question: "Where did the customer go?"

More than two-thirds of all customers who stop buying from a business do so for one reason—they don't feel valued as customers. Although the products may be good, the customer relations aren't. As a result, customers feel ignored and unappreciated. Feeling this way, you'd think they would complain, but they don't. The Office of Consumer Affairs estimates that less than 4 percent of all customers ever bother to complain about what they buy or how they're treated. They just take their business elsewhere; or tell a friend. The average "wronged" customer tells eight to sixteen others about the problem—demonstrating that word-of-mouth publicity can be negative, as well as positive, with the power not only to build your customer franchise, but to tear it down.

By staying in touch you can avoid this, though. If a customer's not happy with something or has a problem, you'll know. And, when the customer's needs change, you'll know that, too.

To help cement your relationships with customers, there are any number of methods you can use to stay in touch, including:

▶ **Telephoning**—not just to solicit orders, but to make contact and let customers know you're only a call away.

▶ **Sending out mailers**—brochures, sales letters, cata-
logues, and announcements of new products, special promotions, or upcoming events.

▶ **Publishing a newsletter** as a service to customers, keeping them posted on the latest news and developments in your
field.

▶ **Sending cards or gifts** at the holidays or on special
occasions to show customers you're thinking about them.

▶ **Sending thank-you notes** expressing your appreciation
for the opportunity to serve customers. This is one of the
most effective methods of all, but you'd be surprised how
few businesses bother to do it.

▶ **Participating in trade shows** where you can touch base
with your current customers and reach out to new ones.

▶ **Networking with customers** through business and professional organizations.

▶ **Taking customers to lunch** to discuss their plans and
assess what their future needs will be.

▶ **Visiting customers regularly** to check on how they're
doing and to give them your latest sales materials.

▶ **Holding an open house** and inviting customers to come
by and meet with you and your team.

▶ **Conducting seminars or training sessions** that provide
customers with needed information.

▶ **Sending electronic messages**—by fax or modem.

▶ **Recording your message**—using audio, video or computer means so customers can play it later.

▶ **Teleconferencing**—saving you and your customers time
while cutting back on travel expenses, too.

▶ **Doing surveys**—to measure customers' satisfaction levels
and get new ideas for ways to serve them.

Whichever methods you use, the important thing is to let customers know that you're there for them and that you *do* value the opportunity to serve them.

Two-Way Communications

Part of being there for customers is making it easy for them to reach you. Communications must be able to flow in both directions—not just from you to customers, but from them to you. To enhance the communication flow and ensure that customers have their say, it helps to:

- ▶ **Have good phone skills.** Make sure that the person who picks up the phone is helpful and efficient. Nothing turns off customers faster than running into a rude operator or being put on hold forever.
- ▶ **Provide a toll-free number.** Customers will feel a lot better about calling you when they know you're paying for the call. Citibank took this suggestion even farther and established a separate 800 number for the hearing-impaired that utilizes teletype phones.
- ▶ **Use beepers.** This way, when a customer has an emergency, the person who's needed can be reached in a hurry.
- ▶ **Use customer response cards.** Give these out to customers at the point of purchase or mail them out later so customers can let you know if they are satisfied with what they received.
- ▶ **Use a suggestion box.** In addition to making it easy for customers to tell you what they're thinking, this provides a visible reminder of your willingness to respond to their needs.

TURNING COMPLAINTS INTO COMPLIMENTS

No matter how good your products or services are, you're bound to get some complaints. You can bank on it. Justified or not, when you're in business, complaints go with the territory; and how you deal with them has a big impact on growth. To hold onto your customers and avoid negative word-of-mouth publicity, your customer relations strategy needs to be directed at resolving any problems that arise and finding ways to keep customers satisfied.

It's important for you to establish guidelines for handling complaints and to make sure that all of your employees know and understand them. As a rule of thumb, when dealing with upset or irate customers it helps to:

► Be a good listener. Let customers voice their displeasure or frustration without cutting them off.
► Make good eye contact and use positive body language.
► Be respectful. Address the customer by name and try to establish a rapport.
► By sympathetic, rather than defensive. Trying to "win" an argument will only result in losing the customer.
► Keep the problem from escalating from a minor complaint into a major castastrophe.
► Thank the customer for bringing the problem to your attention.
► Apologize for any inconvenience the customer is having.
► Get the pertinent information needed to resolve the problem.
► Be honest. If you made a mistake, don't try to cover it up.
► Take care of the problem as quickly as possible. Don't leave the customer waiting indefinitely for a response.
► Keep a record of the complaint and how it was handled.

In most instances, once customers know that you're serious about solving the problem and *do* want to please them, they'll work with you to arrive at a mutually acceptable solution.

Keeping customers satisfied might seem like a lot of work—and it *is*. But in the long run, this is what will enable your business to be successful and to grow even more.

10 | HOW BIG SHOULD YOU GROW?

In growing your business it's important to keep this thought in mind: One size doesn't fit all. Nor does "bigger" always equate with "better." Just as some entrepreneurs favor an aggressive expansion program, others make a conscious effort to keep their businesses small. Each business owner must decide what size best suits his or her business and plan accordingly.

In the words of one retailer, "The most important thing I did in selecting my location was to find a feasible size so that the rent wouldn't kill me. I have seen store after store go down the tubes because it was too big, the rent too high. . . . No matter what you sold, it was never enough." A proponent of small size, she vows to keep her gift shop a size that's "manageable by me."

Contrast that with Richard LaMotta, the inventor of the Chipwich premium ice cream sandwich. For him growth wasn't so much an option as an inevitability. Less than two hours after his vending carts took the streets of New York City to sell his chocolate chip cookies and ice cream creation, all eighteen thousand Chipwich sandwiches were sold out. They didn't have any more and couldn't keep pace with the demand. A second factory was needed . . . immediately. And virtually overnight the "little New York business" LaMotta had initially envisioned was selling its product nationwide, overseas, and on board coast-to-coast airline flights.

An American success story, yes. LaMotta was able to deal with the unexpected growth. But not every entrepreneur would be so fortunate without some sort of strategy to guide the rate and type of expansion that takes place.

FINDING THE RIGHT SIZE

In selecting a course of action—to expand or not to expand—there's more to look at than just the revenues you stand to gain. You'll also want to consider such factors as *cost, efficiency, quality,* and *service.* Will increasing the size of your business have a positive or a negative effect on these areas? The advantage of lower unit costs must be weighed against the disadvantage of higher overhead; the potential for enlarging your market share against the risk of reducing quality and service, and so on.

Cost

At first glane, the costs associated with expanding your business may appear obvious, ranging from the cost of the capital to finance the expansion to the insurance premiums to protect your investment.

COSTS OF EXPANDING:
- Interest on capital
- Remodeling costs
- Construction costs
- Rent/mortgage payments

- Equipment costs
- Furniture costs
- Fixtures costs
- Inventory costs

- Administrative costs
- Selling expenses
- Insurance premiums

But there are other costs, too—the costs of *not* expanding your business. Though less tangible than the first, they are no less important.

COSTS OF NOT EXPANDING:

- *Lost sales* because of an inability to keep up with customer demand
- *Lost market share* because of a failure to compete
- *Higher unit costs* because of inefficient production methods
- *Higher employee turnover costs* because of lack of opportunities for advancement

In other words, it can cost you whether you expand or not. To determine whether further growth will enable your business to be more cost-effective, you must compare both—the costs of expanding and of not expanding—and match them to your projected revenues.

Efficiency

Will expanding your business make it more efficient or less efficient? Enable you to better utilize your resources and reach potential customers? Or take a smoothly running operation and impair its ability to function? It depends on your product offering and your objectives.

Much like the saying, "one man's meat is another man's poison," one entrepreneur's efficiency can be another's undoing. For example, if your goal is to sell clothing to as many people as possible, it makes sense to enlarge your store or add new locations. On the other hand, if you want to stay on the cutting edge of fashion and offer exclusive designs to a select clientele, the answer is less clear. In this instance, expanding could undermine your efficiency, hampering your ability to serve customers' needs and react quickly to changes in the marketplace.

It's also important to note that with increased size comes increased *complexity*—a natural enemy of efficiency. Tasks that were once simple can take on a life of their own as square footage totals and staff counts rise. To achieve greater efficiency your powers of coordination must grow as well. As the British say, it's a matter of "having all your ducks in a row." If you expand your business you must also make provisions to ensure that merchandise is on the shelves, salespeople are ready to sell the goods, and telephone and computer systems are capable of handling the increased transactions.

One high-flying personal computer company found out the importance of coordination the hard way. In a struggle with Apple Computers for market share, the company greatly increased the size of its manufacturing operation, only to have its assembly lines idled while workers waited in vain for suppliers to deliver needed components. While customers' orders backed up, unfinished units stacked up, and the company was forced into backruptcy.

In determining the effect a proposed expansion would have on your efficiency level, attention should be given to such factors as:

▶ The current and future demand for your product offering.
▶ The time needed to carry out each phase of the expansion.
▶ The ability of suppliers to meet your increased needs for goods and services.
▶ The ability of your organization to adapt to the changes.

Quality

A frequent concern in deciding whether to expand is quality control. The larger a business grows, the harder it gets to spot substandard performance or products and take corrective action. To keep growth from hurting quality, entrepreneurs must demonstrate to employees the importance of quality and provide the leadership, training, and incentives needed to achieve it.

To measure the impact that additional expansion would have on quality, ask yourself:

▶ Is my current work force capable of meeting increased operations demands?

▶ Are the resources available to find and train additional workers?

▶ Have quality standards been established and communicated to all?

▶ Are monitoring procedures in place to see that quality levels are maintained?

▶ Is the business making use of new technologies and methods that can improve quality?

▶ Is everyone in the business committed to making quality a top priority?

Since you can't be all places at once, it's essential that you gain employees' support for quality and keep growth at a manageable rate. The stronger your business is in these key areas, the better equipped it will be to accommodate further growth.

▶ Commitment. Quality is seen as a necessity, not a luxury, and workers are committed to maintaining and improving it.

▶ Communication. Employees throughout the business communicate freely with one another and share information readily.
▶ Cooperation. Employees work together in a spirit of cooperation, putting aside barriers and departmental interests.
▶ Contribution. Quality is a common goal with all workers contributing to its achievement.

Service

Like quality, service is an area that can easily suffer when a business expands. With an increase in size, greeting customers by name and catering to individual preferences become more difficult. Instead of offering that "something extra" in the way of service, there's a temptation to standardize products and services and treat all customers alike, regardless of his or her special needs.

In developing a growth startegy, each business must determine the level of service that it wants to provide its customers. The higher the level, the more effort that must go into building customer relationships. It is essential to stay close to the customer. To achieve growth without sacrificing service, you must listen to what customers are telling you and develop ways to track satisfaction.

That's easy to say, but not easy to do. When a business is small the owner can talk to customers and hear their comments firsthand. It's obvious when someone isn't pleased with the service, not only from what's said, but from the *look* on the person's face. But what happens when the second or third or twentieth store opens? Or the business expands to a new state or country? When having a face-to-face dialogue with each customer is no longer possible?

For service to keep pace with growth, two things are critical:

There must be a *communications system* that works, bridging the gap between you and the customer; and *service-oriented employees* able and willing to meet customers' needs.

Ideally, as your business expands, the following service criteria should continue to be met:

▶ Customers can easily reach a business representative when they need to.
▶ Customers' files and records are up-to-date and accessible.
▶ Customers' requests are handled promptly.
▶ Customers' complaints are resolved courteously and efficiently.
▶ Customers are contacted periodically to obtain their inputs.
▶ Customers' needs are anticipated and prepared for in advance.

WAYS TO EXPAND YOUR BUSINESS

After evaluating the preceding factors, if you are still confident that you can expand your business, there are several key ways to approach the growth process. These can be accomplished one at a time, or in combinations.

- Productivity
- Number of employees
- Size of building
- Number of locations
- Licensing and franchising
- Product lines
- Other types of business

Productivity

Borrowing the phrase "work smarter, not harder," you can expand your business by raising productivity and using your current personnel to serve a greater number of customers. Streamlining procedures, automating, and computerizing whenever possible and providing employees with additional training are just some of the ways to increase work capacity without physically expanding the size of your business or adding employees. Replacing outmoded equipment and/or reconfiguring work areas can also boost productivity; so can introducing incentive programs that reward employees for superior performance.

Number of Employees

Adding more employees, full-time, part-time, or "temps," is another way to expand your business. They enable you to serve your current customers better or to accommodate new ones, and don't require any capital expenditures other than for additional equipment or furnishings that may be needed. The main expense here, along with payroll, is the time and money to provide training.

Size of Building

If your current location is bursting at the seams and can't handle more customers or employees, enlarging the size of your building or moving to a bigger site would seem to be in order. Since this option adds to your fixed overhead and may involve incurring long-term debt, look into it closely before going ahead. The main point to consider is whether or not your projected work load justifies the increased capacity. For example, if sales drop off or anticipated increases aren't realized, will you still need the extra space? A common mistake businesses make is to get a big order or have an exceptionally good season and expand on that basis, not realizing that this is a windfall, rather than the norm.

Number of Locations

Another way to expand your business is to use multiple locations. Involving both capital expenditures and an increase in your fixed overhead, this type of expansion has several variations, including:

▶ SETTING UP A SEPARATE WAREHOUSE so that the majority of your existing space can be used for selling and administrative activities. Since warehouse space is generally less expensive this should reduce your inventory carrying costs.

▶ HAVING A CENTRAL HEADQUARTERS where administration and planning take place and utilizing geographically dispersed show rooms or sales offices where merchandise is displayed.

▶ ESTABLISHING A CHAIN OF LOCATIONS (known as a "horizontal combination"), with each location offering essentially the same products or services.

HORIZONTAL COMBINATION

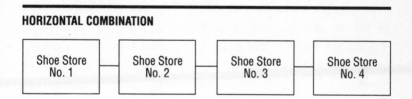

The advantages of these methods are that they can enable you to serve your current target market more efficiently or to branch out into new markets, expanding to other cities, states, or countries. The downside is the increased costs involved and the risk of having a poorly performing location bring down your overall profits.

One retailer who found a way to deal with both of these problems is Mrs. Fields. In addition to the cookie chain's familiar mall locations, it began using small kiosks and mobile stands that it can pick up and move when demand levels shift.

Licensing and Franchising

Licensing and franchising (which is discussed in the next chapter) are ways to expand your business without adding to your payroll or fixed costs. This is because, in both situations, you're granting someone else the right to do business by utilizing your name or other assets belonging to you. As a result, the person or business receiving this right not only incurs the various costs involved, but pays you a predetermined fee and/or percentage of the profits.

Licensing, which is the simpler of the two arrangements, entails letting someone produce goods or offer services that utilize your technology (designs, patents, recipes, etc.) or bear your name, trademark, likeness, endorsement, or other symbol. For example, license-holders are permitted to imprint the Coca-Cola company's name and trademark on an array of products ranging from clothing to housewares.

Franchising takes this one step farther; authorizing franchises to set up and operate businesses patterned on your own, utilizing your name, trademark, processes, procedures, and so on. Although these separate business units look and function the same as company-owned chain stores, the difference is that they are run by independent owner-operators, rather than by managers.

In determining whether to use either of these methods, your primary concern should be to ensure that nothing is done to damage the reputation of your business. This means entering into licensing or franchising agreements carefully and keeping a close watch on the product offerings that bear your name.

Product Lines

Rather than making more of the same product, expanding your product line increases the size of your business by creating something new. This enables you to reach new customers or sell to your existing ones—*again*. It's the same method the major soap companies use to sell more soaps and detergents—making them available in a variety of forms for dishes, laundry, face and hands, shampoo, and so on.

In exploring this option, you can offer:

▶ A SINGLE PRODUCT LINE with variations of the same product—shampoo for dry, normal, oily, and processed hair. The more products you offer, the *deeper* the line is said to be.

or

▶ MULTIPLE PRODUCT LINES (known collectively as a "product mix") with different categories, or lines, of products—shampoo, rinses, conditioners, hair colorings, and so on. The more product lines you have, the *wider* the mix; the more products within each line, the *deeper* the mix.

The main advantage of adding new products or lines is that this lets you trade on your existing resources and name identity. Customers who are already satisfied with your current product offering should be receptive to the additions. Since the new products will reflect on the old, though, it's essential for their quality to be up to your standards. Otherwise, you run the risk of hurting your entire product group.

Other Types of Business

The most complicated and generally costly method of expansion is to branch out into another type of business. Like expanding your product line, this approach involves creating something new, but in this case, instead of a new product, it's a new business.

One way to do this is to form a *vertical combination*. This means expanding your business to encompass the production or distribution activities that are related to it but currently performed by others.

VERTICAL COMBINATION

In the example shown, the owner of the shoe store not only sells shoes, but manufactures and wholesales them as well. A combination like this can originate from the bottom up, from the top down, or even from the middle. Thus the retailer could start the manufacturing plant to guarantee a supply of shoes for the shoe store; the manufacturer could open the shoe store to provide a retail outlet for its shoes; or the wholesaler could expand in both directions to take over the entire production-distribution process.

Another way to branch out into a different type of business is to form a *conglomerate*—a combination of unrelated businesses such as a chain of shoe stores, a food processing company, a health club, and a magazine. Although primarily associated with Big Business, this method could be employed by smaller businesses seeking to enter new fields.

A conglomerate is probably the riskiest of the expansion methods described, since, in addition to its cost, it entails becoming proficient in more than one industry. However, because this strategy allows you to put your eggs in more than one basket, it can also reduce your risk when profits are down in one area.

Considering the various ways to expand your business, you could conceivably select one or all of them. Naturally, if you increase the number of your locations or branch out into other types of business, the number of employees you need also increases. In expanding your product line it may be necessary to expand the size of your building as well, to provide additional manufacturing or selling space. In other words, the decision to expand in one area may require you to expand in another area, too. Just as changing one face on a Rubik's Cube changes another, each method of expansion affects the others.

CONGLOMERATE

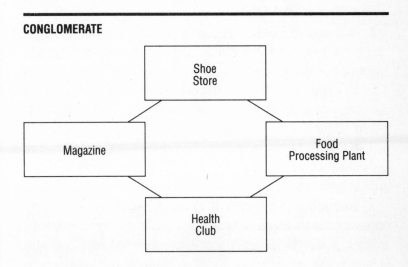

ENTERING FOREIGN MARKETS

As high-tech communications and improved transportation methods combine to shrink distances, the world is fast becoming a global marketplace with more and more businesses expanding by entering foreign markets. And with two-thirds of the world's potential customers outside the United States, it makes sense to consider getting involved in international marketing.

Some of the advantages of expanding internationally include:

1. **Broadening your customer base.** By going outside the U.S., you can reach additional customers with a need for your product offering.

2. **Extending your product's life cycle.** A product that has reached its peak in the U.S. may be just starting to catch on in another country.

3. **Stabilizing sales.** Selling in other countries can help to keep downturns in domestic demand from having as great an impact on your sales levels.

4. **Achieving economies of scale.** By serving a larger target market you can increase your production volume and lower your unit costs.

5. **Selling off excess inventory.** Inventory that would otherwise be in storage can be sold in markets where there is a demand for it.

6. **Raising profit margins.** The cost or pricing structures associated with doing business in another country may be more profitable than the U.S.

7. **Reducing government restrictions.** Since laws and regulations pertaining to business vary from one country to another, it may be easier to manufacture or sell your products in foreign markets.

8. **Utilizing tax breaks.** The U.S. and foreign governments often offer tax breaks or other incentives to promote international trade.

The advantages notwithstanding, entrepreneurs should exercise caution in making the decision to engage in international marketing. The time and expense it takes to overcome logistics, language, and other barriers can be substantial. Among the factors you'll want to consider are:

▶ Your current financial position
▶ Your production capability
▶ The marketing skills of your personnel
▶ The demand for your product offering
▶ Your projected revenues and expenses
▶ The competition you would face
▶ The characteristics of each market:
  geographic, demographic, political/legal, economic, social/cultural, technological

The more secure your business is in its current markets and the more knowledge you have of the foreign markets you are seeking to enter, the better your chances of success. This means taking the time to (1) assess strengths and weaknesses of your business and (2) gather information on each country viewed as a potential market for your goods or services.

As shown in the following listing, there are many sources of information you can use to obtain marketing research data.

U.S. GOVERNMENT

Agency for International Development Washington, D.C. 20523	Administers U.S. foreign economic assistance programs; helps put American businesses in touch with foreign buyers in receipt of aid.
Department of Commerce Washington, D.C. 20230	Maintains a global network of trade specialists; oversees trade opportunities programs; prepares reports and surveys on international business conditions.

Department of State Washington, D.C. 20520	Has personnel in the U.S. and at embassies and consulates in over 140 countries; provides advice, marketing research data, and assistance in making foreign contacts.
International Trade Administration Washington, D.C. 20230	Provides information and assistance in all areas of foreign trade; works closely with industries, trade associations, and state development agencies to open up foreign markets; maintains Country Desks providing research data from offices around the world.
Small Business Administration Washington, D.C. 20416	Provides counseling, advice, training, and publications on international marketing; maintains an export/import data base on product sales worldwide; matches businesses with agents and foreign distributors.
U.S. Trade Representative Washington, D.C. 20501	Coordinates U.S. trade policy and negotiates agreements; provides information on trade related matters, laws, regulations, and tariffs.

INTERNATIONAL ORGANIZATIONS

Organization of Economic Cooperation and Development Washington, D.C. 20036	Promotes the economic and social welfare of the 24 countries that make up the organization's membership; prepares publications on each country's economy, exports/imports, local industries, tourism, etc.
United Nations New York, N.Y. 10017	Administers various programs that provide information and assistance on international trade; compiles statistics and monitors economic trends.
World Bank Washington, D.C. 20433	Provides economic assistance to developing nations; advises U.S. businesses of foreign contracting opportunities available in conjunction with its aid programs.

| World Trade Centers Association New York, N.Y. 10048 | Has over 160 world trade centers located in cities around the world; maintains an on-line international data link; provides information on foreign markets, regulations, and tariffs; holds educational seminars. |

OTHER SOURCES

American Chambers of Commerce Abroad
Commercial Bank International Departments
Foreign Consulates and Trade Offices in the United States
Trade and Professional Associations

PUBLICATIONS

A Basic Guide to Exporting
U.S. Government Printing Office.
A manual covering all facets of international trade, market research, and
    stragegy.

Business America
U.S. Government Printing Office.
Biweekly magazine on international trade issues and business opportunities
    overseas.

International Trade Statistics Yearbook
Published by the United Nations.
Provides trade statistics by region, country, and product classification.

World Factbook
U.S. Government Printing Office.
Country-by-country data on government, economy, geography, people,
    communications, etc.

When it comes to actually taking the plunge and entering the international marketplace, there are several entry strategies from which to choose. As you can see from the chart that follows, the level of investment and risk associated with each strategy ranges from low to high.

Exporting/Importing

The most common foreign entry strategy utilized by American businesses is importing and exporting. This entails the least

INTERNATIONAL MARKETING ENTRY STRATEGIES

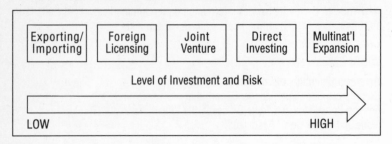

amount of effort, money, and risk. Basically it calls for you to either sell (export) or buy (import) goods or services in a foreign market. Providing you with outlets for your merchandise or sources of supply for your current markets, this method encompasses such activities as finding buyers or sellers, negotiating payment terms, and making shipping arrangements. If you choose, much of this can be handled by an agent or export management company in exchange for a commission. And, since no investment is made abroad, your risk of loss is primarily limited to the value of the goods being traded.

Foreign Licensing

Like licensing in the United States, this entry strategy involves authorizing another business to manufacture a product using your name, technology, patents, or other assets while enabling you to receive royalty payments. The appeal of this strategy is that it doesn't require investing any capital or performing manufacturing or marketing activities. What makes it more involved than exporting or importing, though, is the time needed to build relationships with licensees. The main drawback is the difficulty in maintaining quality control over the goods that are produced.

Joint Venture

Taking licensing one step farther, a joint venture involves joining with local investors to form and operate a business in a foreign country. A popular strategy with businesses, large and small, this reduces the risk of investing in another country by getting a partner to share the risk. Pooling money, skills, marketing information, and other resources, you and your partner work together as a team. Aside from lowering the amount of the investment capital needed to establish a foreign operation, this has two other distinct advantages: (1) it enables you to meet foreign governments' requirements that part of your business be locally owned and (2) it provides you with a partner who knows the tastes and culture of the country. The main disadvantages of a joint venture are the potential for conflicts between partners and the commitment of time and money that must be made.

Direct Investment

Riskier than a joint venture, a direct investment strategy calls for you to go it alone, establishing a foreign business by yourself, retaining full ownership. In this case you would be investing in facilities and equipment and incurring all the labor costs and other expenses associated with the operation. The advantages of this approach are the opportunity to (1) avoid government tariffs on imports, (2) exert more control over the business, (3) maintain a bigger presence in the country, and (4) build goodwill among foreign consumers. The downside, of course, is the high level of financial commitment it requires; and if a problem arises in the country (government instability, economic decline, currency fluctuation, etc.), your entire investment could be jeopardized.

Multinational Expansion

The riskiest strategy of all, but offering the greatest potential rewards, is to expand on a multinational level. A business adopting this expansion method views the whole world as its market and maintains bases of operation around the globe. Rather than sending goods *to* foreign markets, it is *part* of the markets, with facilities, sales offices, and personnel operating within the countries. Seeing itself not so much as an "American company," but as a company of the world, a multinational company (MNC) often owns shares in foreign businesses and has foreign investors who own shares in it. Depending on the degree to which it sees a universal demand for its product offering, an MNC will utilize one of two marketing approaches:

- ▶ **A multinational marketing strategy** that recognizes the differences among countries and develops individual product offerings customized to meet the needs of each market; or
- ▶ **A global marketing strategy** that treats the world as a single market with common characteristics and develops a standard product offering designed to meet all needs.

This last foreign entry strategy normally evolves out of one of the earlier ones, coming about as companies grow and develop a better feel for the international marketplace. Drawing heavily on both your resources and powers of coordination, it requires your full commitment to succeed.

11 | THE FRANCHISE QUESTION

Franchising can provide the influx of capital and people necessary to turn a small business into a giant operation. But if you aren't careful, it can also be the undoing of an already successful business, undermining the consistency and quality of your products or services. Whether franchising is the way to go depends on the individual characteristics of each business—and each business owner. In exploring this option it's important to ask yourself, "Will franchising be a fast track to riches or a costly detour?"

If you elect to expand your business through franchising, as the *franchisor* you will be allowing independent business persons, the *franchisees,* to produce and/or market your company's products or services. In exchange for a fee, each franchisee will have the right to use your company's name, trademarks, service marks, processes, and sales and marketing methods to run his or her business, the *franchise.*

A kind of licensing agreement, franchising enables franchisors to obtain the money and manpower they need to grow a business without having to go into debt, sell stock, or hire additional employees. Instead of laying out funds, franchisors *receive* them—and get motivated workers, to boot—making it possible to open and run more business units. The franchisees, in turn, get to capitalize on the parent company's success and to make use of the various resources (training, financing, promotion, and assistance) the franchisor provides. Rather than spending months, or even years, starting a business from scratch, they are already running one.

It sounds like a marriage made in heaven, right? And it *can* be. For franchising to work, though, it must be mutually beneficial for the franchisor *and* the franchisees. Both parties must feel that the advantages of franchising outweigh the disadvantages. Then, and only then, can you begin to fully utilize this method of business expansion.

FRANCHISING'S ADVANTAGES AND DISADVANTAGES

To accurately assess the advantages and disadvantages of franchising your business, it's essential to look at it from both viewpoints—the franchisor's and the franchisee's.

The Advantages to the Franchisor:

Rapid business expansion is possible with minimal outlays of capital. This enables you to save the time and money that otherwise would be spent lining up financing and recruiting employees.

Franchisors receive an ongoing flow of revenues. These come in the form of franchise fees, royalty payments, and various charges for promotion, financing, and other benefits.

Investment risks are lower. By having the franchisees themselves finance your business expansion, your risk of financial loss is significantly reduced.

There's more time for long-range planning. Since franchisees are responsible for the day-to-day aspects of running their franchises, you are free to focus on the "big picture" and the development of company-wide policies and strategies.

Economies of scale can be achieved. As the size of your business grows, the unit costs of producing its goods or services should come down.

Franchised operations have increased purchasing power and promotional clout. Through bulk-buying and cooperative advertising campaigns that promote the franchise organization as a whole, franchisors get "more bang for the buck."

Franchisees are highly motivated. Since each franchisee has a personal stake invested in your business, you can count on them to do everything possible to make the business succeed.

Franchisees generally have a strong entrepreneurial drive. Attracted by the opportunity to "be the boss," franchisees can be expected to show initiative—rather than waiting to be "told" what to do, they'll *do* it.

The Disadvantages to the Franchisor:

Franchisors have less control over franchisees than they do over employees. Rather than saying, "my way or the highway," you must be willing to work as a team with your franchisees and to give them a say in how the franchise operation is run.

Franchisees may be lacking in the skills needed to operate their businesses successfully. One of your responsibilities as a franchisor will be to provide franchisees with ongoing training and assistance.

A poorly run franchise makes the entire franchise organization look bad. Just as a chain is only as strong as its weakest link, so is a franchise organization only as good as its worst member—proper selection and training of franchisees is critical.

It takes time to set up and oversee a franchise operation. You may find that the time saved in expanding your business this way is overshadowed by the increased administrative duties you'll have to perform.

If a franchise isn't working out, it can be difficult to sever the relationship. Unlike a manager, who is an employee, franchisees are independent owner-operators and, as such, have specific rights concerning termination procedures that must be spelled out in the franchise agreement.

The costs associated with franchising a business can be greater than expected. Along with the attorney and accountant fees to put the franchise operation together and comply with government disclosure requirements are the ongoing legal, administrative, and training costs.

There's less privacy. Federal and state laws require each franchisor to provide prospective franchisees and the public at large with extensive information pertaining to the franchise operation, the persons affiliated with it, and its legal and financial dealings.

The Advantages to the Franchisee:

The business is "ready-made." Franchisees are essentially buying a "turnkey" operation with an existing product and marketing strategy already in place.

There's a lower risk of failure. The instant name recognition that the franchisor provides, coupled with the ongoing assistance and training, gives franchisees an edge over other businesses without those resources.

Promotional strength is greater. In addition to benefiting from the parent organization's national advertising, franchisees can pool their advertising dollars to do joint promotions.

Attracting customers is easier. Customers who are already

sold on the franchise operation as a whole should be sold on the franchise as well.

Financial support is often provided. It's not uncommon for franchisors to help finance the initial start-up costs and to offer advice in the areas of money management and accounting.

Group buying power keeps costs down. Franchisees can often buy the things they need to run their businesses directly from the franchisor, who buys in bulk for the group and passes the savings along.

It's a team effort. Rather than going it alone and learning how to run a business through trial and error, franchisees are part of a team with access to the shared experiences and support of the franchisor and other franchisees.

The Disadvantages to the Franchisee:

There's less freedom. Since the terms of the franchise agreement must be followed, franchisees aren't always free to run their businesses the way they choose.

The price may be too high. When the start-up costs, continuing charges, and royalty payments are added up, prospective franchisees may find themselves priced out of the franchise market.

The franchisor controls the transfer of ownership. The right to transfer ownership of the business to someone else is generally restricted by the franchisor, whose approval is needed before title to the franchise can change hands.

Products or services can't be changed at will. Franchisees aren't allowed to add or drop products, alter recipes or procedures, or otherwise modify their product offerings without the franchisor's permission—even if their way is better.

The franchise's reputation is affected by other franchise members. No matter how good an individual franchise is, if customers have bad experiences at other outlets in the franchisor's organization, they'll assume that *all* the outlets are bad.

Running a franchise is time-consuming. It not only entails overseeing the daily operation, but also being on call to handle problems that arise (such as filling in for an absent employee) and taking care of paperwork.

In looking at franchising from both viewpoints given here, you must determine whether the advantages for you, as the franchisor, more than compensate for the disadvantages. You must also assess your ability to satisfy franchisees' needs and to live up to their expectations of what a franchisor should be.

EIGHT CRITICAL QUESTIONS

Once you've considered the advantages and disadvantages franchising has to offer, you're ready to look at it from the perspective of your particular business. Having examined the overall concept, it's time to ask yourself these eight questions:

1. Can my business be duplicated in other locations?
2. Can others be trained to run businesses patterned on mine?
3. Is it economically feasible to franchise my business?
4. Can adequate controls be enforced to protect my business if it is franchised?
5. Would franchising have a positive effect on the image of my business?
6. Is there sufficient customer demand to justify franchising my business?
7. Do I have enough experience running my business to take on the added responsibility of managing a franchise network?
8. Will franchising enable me to achieve my objectives?

1. Can my business be duplicated in other locations?
To be a good candidate for franchising, your business must be one that can be successfully duplicated in other locations. A

business that caters to the special needs of one community or utilizes materials and equipment that aren't readily available elsewhere will be more difficult to franchise than one that is less specialized. The more universal the appeal of your product offering, the better.

2. Can others be trained to run businesses patterned on mine?

The more education, skills, or experience required to run your business, the harder it will be to franchise it. It's easier to train someone to run a restaurant or change an automobile muffler than to train someone to create an original artwork or program a computer. Businesses calling for workers with basic skills that can be easily learned or taught tend to fare the best. For more complex businesses, such as accounting services or real estate brokerages, *simplification* is the key—developing standardized procedures and breaking down tasks into simple activities that can be performed by workers with average skills.

3. Is it economically feasible to franchise my business?

In the beginning the costs of meeting state and federal regulations, preparing contracts, advertising, training franchisees, and traveling from one franchise location to another can be staggering. Before attempting to franchise your business, it's important to have a solid financial base on which to build. If your business is having financial difficulties, adding franchises may do more harm than good, diverting resources that could go to strengthening it. The financial health of your business is only half the equation, though. You must also look at the economy as a whole (consumer spending, employment levels, interest rates, etc.) to determine if the timing is right.

4. Can adequate controls be enforced to protect my business if it is franchised?

Since the actions of one franchisee reflect on all the others, maintaining adequate control over the entire franchise operation is crucial to your success. Your business must lend itself to standardized procedures and policies that can be enforced for the good of all franchise members. The more you are able to *quantify* what's expected of franchisees (i.e., hours of operation, specific activities to be carried out) and what the product offering will consist of (a standard-sized bag of french fries, the steps included in a beauty facial), the easier it will be to monitor performance and maintain quality.

5. Would franchising have a positive effect on the image of my business?

In considering franchising's effect on your business operation, also consider its effect on your company's image. If your business is known for its one-of-a-kind products or personalized service, franchising's broader marketing approach might detract from that image of exclusivity. Here the challenge is to reach out to a wider group of consumers without alienating your current target market.

6. Is there sufficient customer demand to justify franchising my business?

Increasing the size of your operation through franchising calls for increasing your customer base as well. It's important to determine in advance whether the potential demand for your product or service is large enough to support a franchise network. Unless the numbers are there you're better off with a more targeted means of expansion, such as opening additional company-owned stores in key markets, to reach new customers.

7. Do I have enough experience running my business to take on the added responsibility of managing a franchise network?

Business owners in a hurry to capitalize on a hot idea or get the jump on the competition sometimes rush into franchising before they are ready for it, often with disastrous results. It's a good idea to wait until you have had enough time to get used to running your existing business before taking on others.

8. Will franchising enable me to achieve my objectives?

Developing a franchise network requires a high level of commitment on the part of the franchisor. You'll be investing large amounts of time and money into it. Before deciding to franchise your business, ask yourself whether you're willing to pay the price and whether this method is compatible with your objectives—professionally and personally.

PUTTING TOGETHER A FRANCHISING TEAM

Based on your answers to the preceding questions, if you feel confident that franchising is right for you, the next step is to assemble your franchising team—the people who will help launch and sustain your new venture.

At a minimum, you will need the services of a competent *accountant* and *attorney* to handle the financial and legal aspects associated with creating a franchise operation. You may also want to utilize a *marketing consultant* to assist you in reaching prospective franchisees, a *training specialist* to help franchisees develop the skills needed to run their businesses, and/or an *advertising agency* to promote your organization. These last three, while helpful, aren't essential. Whether you add them to your team depends on your budget, the size of your franchise operation, and your ability to do the work yourself or with existing employees.

Choosing an Accountant

Needless to say your accountant must be familiar with the current IRS regulations pertaining to franchise operations and the requirements for reporting initial franchise fees and subsequent payments. Along with this, it's important that the accountant know how to set up the various impound accounts required by the states in which you do business. Your accountant should be able to assist you in determining your capitalization needs and in projecting annual revenues and expenses.

Choosing an Attorney

To conform to government regulations and prepare the required disclosure document and franchise agreement, there's no getting around the need for an attorney—not just any attorney, but one experienced in franchise law. Your attorney must be capable of helping you to determine fees and payment schedules, setting forth the rights and responsibilities for you and your franchisees, and advising you on various legal matters.

Choosing a Marketing Consultant

As your franchise operation grows, it may be to your advantage to hire a marketing consultant to assist in handling information requests from prospective franchisees and in developing your marketing plan. A consultant can help you to identify people who would make good franchisees and to contact them through business opportunity magazines, newspaper classifieds, trade shows, and other means. If you use a consultant, though, make sure that the person you choose is aware of the legal restrictions governing the sale of franchises.

Choosing a Training Specialist

Given your obligation to provide franchisees with continuing training and guidance, adding a training specialist to your team could easily become a top priority. In order for your franchise operation to succeed, individual franchisees must succeed, which means not only knowing how to produce a product or perform a service, but having strong sales and management skills. Training is the key—through manuals, audio and video tapes, seminars, workshops, and other programs. McDonald's, a leader in training, has even gone so far as to establish its "Hamburger University" to teach franchisees the fine art of fast-food preparation and sales.

Choosing an Advertising Agency

To create national advertising campaigns and assist franchisees in developing their own local promotions, an advertising agency can be invaluable. Since one of the main advantages of buying a franchise is the name recognition that comes with it, franchisees will expect you to actively promote the company. Unless you or your staff are skilled in this area, you'll need an advertising agency to produce ads, obtain media placements, oversee sales promotions (contests, premiums, coupons, etc.), and coordinate your promotion activities.

WHAT TO LOOK FOR IN A FRANCHISEE

Finding good franchisees takes time and effort. It's not just a matter of finding someone who's willing to sign on the dotted line and put your company's name over the door. A good franchisee has certain characteristics that set him or her apart from the pack. Among those characteristics most often cited are

1. **Hard working.** Naturally you want someone who is willing to work as hard as it takes to make the franchise succeed. A person who expects to "get rich quick" or own a business that "runs itself" isn't likely to be much of an asset.

2. **Has business knowledge.** Preferably a franchisee should possess basic business skills—knowledge of sales, management, bookkeeping, computers, etc. Having worked in a similar franchise before is another plus; although persons lacking in these areas shouldn't be ruled out if they are eager to learn and to acquire the skills they need.

3. **Highly motivated.** Franchisees must *want* to be successful. Rather than someone who says, "If it doesn't work out, I'll do something else," you want someone who will *make* it work.

4. **Has adequate financing.** A franchisee needs to have enough start-up capital to keep the business going until it becomes self-sustaining. Close scrutiny of applicants' financial statements is crucial to avoid having franchisees run into money problems later.

5. **A team player.** Franchisees must be willing to follow instructions and run their businesses in accordance with the franchise agreement.

6. **Creative.** Contradictory as it may seem, it is also important for franchisees to be creative and to put their own personal touches on their franchises, coming up with ways to improve the product or service they provide. Rather than attempting to stifle creativity, franchisors should *harness* it, for the good of the entire operation.

7. **Likes people.** Since running a franchise involves countless daily interactions with others—customers, employees, suppliers, headquarters personnel—it also helps if franchisees enjoy being around people. Good human relations skills and a genuine desire to satisfy the customer are a critical part of the franchisee's makeup.

THE LEGAL SIDE OF FRANCHISING

To avoid running into legal problems, you and your attorney will need to be familiar with the various federal and state regulations that apply to franchising. The most all-encompassing of these is the Trade Regulation Rule enacted by the Federal Trade Commission. In accordance with this rule, franchisors are required to provide a *disclosure document* revealing the franchisor's background, the financial status of the company, terms of the franchise agreement, and so on. By law, prospective franchisees must receive this document, also known as the Uniform Franchise Offering Circular (UFOC), or simply, the "offering circular," at their first personal meeting with you or your representative and no less than ten business days before they sign an agreement or make any payment on the franchise.

The Disclosure Document

Consisting of twenty categories in all, a disclosure document must furnish prospective franchisees with the following FTC-required information:

1. Identifying information about the franchisor.
2. Business experience of the franchisor's directors and key executives.
3. The franchisor's business experience.

4. Litigation history of the franchisor and its directors and key executives.
5. Bankruptcy history of the franchisor and its directors and key executives.
6. Description of the franchise.
7. Money required to be paid by the franchisee to obtain or commence the franchise operation.
8. Continuing expenses to the franchisee in operating the franchise business that are payable in whole or in part to the franchisor.
9. A list of persons who are either the franchisor or any of its affiliates with whom the franchisee is required or advised to do business.
10. Realty, personalty, services, etc., which the franchisee is required to purchase, lease, or rent and a list of any persons from whom such transactions must be made.
11. Description of consideration paid (such as royalties, commissions, etc.) by third parties to the franchisor or any of its affiliates as a result of a franchisee's purchase from such third parties.
12. Description of any franchisor assistance in financing the purchase of a franchise.
13. Restrictions placed on a franchisor's conduct of its business.
14. Required personal participation by the franchisee.
15. Termination, cancellation, and renewal of the franchise.
16. Statistical information about the number of franchises and their rate of terminations.
17. Franchisor's right to select or approve a site for the franchise.
18. Training programs for the franchisee.
19. Celebrity involvement with the franchise.
20. Financial information about the franchisor.

As soon as your disclosure document is complete and your franchising team is in place, you can get your franchise operation under way. In so doing, though, keep in mind that this is a pivotal transition not only for your business, but for you as well. Having been an entrepreneur, you must now take on the added role of mentor. In addition to growing your own business, you must be prepared to help others grow theirs.

12 PUBLIC OR PRIVATE?

What entrepreneur hasn't dreamed of going public one day? Of selling shares of stock on the open market and watching their price climb through the stratosphere? Of gaining instant access to investment capital? Of becoming rich overnight? It happens. But the journey from initial public offering to *Fortune* magazine cover isn't quite as linear as the dream would have you believe.

Taking a company public is an accomplishment in itself—an involved and lengthy process that not all businesses are equipped or advised to attempt. Nor is there any guarantee that, having gone public, a business will be any better off than it was before. Thus, in considering this growth strategy, you must weigh the pros and cons carefully.

THE PROS AND CONS

Offering shares of stock in your business to the general public has these advantages:

Increased Access to Capital

By letting the investing public at large buy stock in your business, you can raise substantial sums of capital without having to draw on your own resources or take on debt. This not only reduces your personal risk, but cuts down on the cost of funds, since investment capital doesn't have to be repaid and is interest-free.

Personal Income and Liquidity

Going public puts a market value on your ownership stake in the business and provides a way to convert your equity into cash by either selling some of your personal holdings or borrowing against them.

Easier Transfer of Ownership

When your business is publicly traded, it is much easier for investors to buy and sell shares of stock in it, transferring ownership at will, rather than having to go through private placements. As a result, your stock becomes more desirable and your pool of potential investors expands.

Motivated Employees

A publicly traded company often has an advantage when it comes to attracting and keeping employees since it can offer them stock in the business. In addition to giving employees a feeling of ownership, this gives them the opportunity to build wealth through stock price increases and tax savings.

Improved Expansion Capabilities

It takes money to expand and, often, the only way to raise enough of it, fast enough, is by broadening your investor base to include the general public. What's more, if you want to acquire or merge with another company, having stock with a proven market value strengthens your negotiating position and gives you the option of using the stock, rather than cash, to finance the expansion.

Easier Retirement and Estate Planning

When it comes to retirement and estate planning, having a publicly traded company makes it easier to obtain cash when you need it, and to transfer assets to others through gifts and bequests. And, since stock is highly liquid, there's less danger of your heirs being forced to sell or break up the business to raise money to pay inheritance taxes.

On the other hand going public has these disadvantages:

Lack of Secrecy

The main disadvantage is the legal requirement that publicly owned companies must disclose sensitive information about their operations and objectives to shareholders, the government, and others. For example, you would have to reveal such information as executive salaries and stock option plans; sales revenues, gross margins and profits; investments and borrowings.

Loss of Control

Investors who buy stock in your company aren't just buying a piece of paper, but a piece of the business. As such, they will expect to have a say in how it is run. To avoid losing the deciding voice in making decisions, it's important that you keep enough stock to retain management control. The more widely dispersed the shares of stock are, the less shares you'll need. On the other hand, if the shares are narrowly dispersed among just a few parties, you will need more to stay in control.

Performance Pressures

Shareholders can be very demanding when rating the performance of a business, expecting it to achieve steady growth in sales, profits, and stock price regardless of the marketing environment. The constant pressure to meet shareholder expectations can take its toll, causing stress and anxiety, forcing you to focus on making short-term gains, rather than accomplishing long-term objectives.

Increased Costs

The costs of preparing an initial public offering (IPO) and registering and selling the stock, as well as meeting the ongoing reporting requirements once your business has gone public, can be considerable. Good legal and accounting services don't come cheap (the bills can mount up quickly), and administrative and public relations costs have to be factored in. To avoid a financial fiasco it's essential to work from a detailed budget and keep a close watch on expenses.

Added Time Expenditures

Going public takes a tremendous amount of time to get all the financial and disclosure documents in order, meet with securities analysts and potential investors, and keep shareholders informed of your activities. Running the business itself can become almost incidental. To stay on top of everything, you'll need lots of stamina and a strong management team.

EVALUATING YOUR POSITION

In addition to looking at the pros and cons associated with going public, you must also evaluate your business's current position in terms of its readiness and ability to make a successful public offering. Among the key points to consider are:

- The business's focus
- How well the business is functioning
- The rate of sales growth
- Future growth trends
- Your competitive advantages
- Your product development activities
- Investment appeal
- Available resources

The business's focus. Have you adequately answered the question "What business am I in?", determining which products or services you want to sell, to which target markets. If your business is still going through the process of finding itself, you're better off waiting until your identity and objectives are clear before making a public offering.

How well the business is functioning. Is your business running smoothly enough to weather the disruptions of a public offering and the added scrutiny that goes with it? While top management is concentrating on getting the stock issued and courting investors, the day-to-day activities of the business still need to be carried out. To keep things going, it's critical that you have people you can count on to mind the store.

The rate of sales growth. Have you been able to build and sustain increasing sales? One of the primary things investors look for in a new stock issue is a track record of rising sales with an annual growth rate of 25 percent or higher.

Future growth trends. What do you expect future sales to be? If you can demonstrate to investors that the market for your products or services is expanding, half the battle is won. A business that is in a growth industry has a much better chance of attracting investors than one that is in a declining industry.

Your competitive advantages. What is there about your product offering that makes it better than the competition's? To hold your own in the marketplace and convince investors that you're a good risk, you must have something everyone else doesn't—a patented product, a recognizable name, better service, more efficient distribution, lower prices, or other advantages.

Your product development activities. What's on the drawing board? Once your business goes public, investors will be counting on you to deliver the goods. This means being able to meet the demand for your existing products and to create new ones. Since consumers' needs are constantly changing, it's important for you to be able to keep pace with them, modifying and improving your products and expanding your product line.

Investment appeal. Does your business have the kind of chemistry that turns investors on? A strong income statement and balance sheet are very appealing, of course. But, there's more to it than that. Investors also rate a business on such factors as management strength, position in the industry, customer acceptance, image, and so on.

Available resources. Do you have everything you need to go the distance? Taking a company public requires time, money, and personnel. And once the stock is sold the real work begins—satisfying your shareholders. To carry out all the tasks that must be done you'll need sufficient resources and have to allocate them well.

GOING PUBLIC

If you think that going public is in the best interest of your business then you should begin to lay the groundwork. Preparing and marketing an initial public offering is a complicated process and there are specific steps that you must follow.

Steps in the Initial Public Offering Process (IPO)

1. **Assess your team.** Take an objective look at your management personnel and outside attorneys and accountants to determine if they possess the necessary experience and abilities to launch a successful IPO. It takes special skills to guide a company through the IPO process, and you may find that additional help is needed or that replacements have to be made.

2. **Put your records in order.** Since both the government and the public will be going over your records with a fine-tooth comb, it's critical that they be in perfect condition. You'll need detailed financial statements showing past revenues, expenses, taxable income, assets and liabilities, and the legal documents pertaining to your organizational structure, agreements and obligations, patents and trademarks, and so on.

3. **Choose an underwriter.** The underwriter is the investment banking firm who will oversee the stock offering. In effect, the quarterback for your team, the underwriter has the job to advise you of the best time to go public and to price and sell the securities.

4. **Prepare the registration statement.** Once you've gotten everything and everyone in place, you're ready to go to work on preparing the registration statement required by the Securities and Exchange Commission. As shown in the outline on page 165, it consists of two main parts. The first part (also

called the "prospectus") contains the core information about your business and goes to potential investors. The second part contains supplemental information and doesn't have to go to investors, although they can see it upon request.

5. **File the registration statement.** When you've completed both parts of your statement, the next step is to file it with the SEC for review. The agency will determine if it meets all of the requirements and cite any deficiencies that exist.

6. **Distribute copies of the prospectus.** While you're waiting to hear from the SEC (usually within 30 days) you can go ahead and send out copies of your prospectus to potential investors. This preliminary prospectus is called a "red herring," because a notice in red must appear on its front cover warning investors that the securities haven't been approved by the SEC and are not currently for sale. The red herring's function is to gauge the level of interest in the IPO.

7. **Meet with investors.** During the waiting period, you and your team can begin to meet with institutional investors and securities analysts to tell them about your business. Known as a "dog and pony show," this entails going on the road to the main cities where your stock will be traded and generating support for the new issue.

8. **Coordinate state filings.** In addition to getting the SEC's approval to market your securities, you must also have the offering "qualified" in those states where it will be sold. These include the states where the greatest numbers of investors are likely to be found as well as the states where your business has facilities or conducts operations.

9. **Set the price.** Once the revised registration statement has been approved by the SEC and the filing is complete it's time to set the price for the offering. This is when you and the underwriter must determine what investors are willing to pay. A calculation based as much on marketing savvy as on mathe-

matics, the price you arrive at will have a major bearing on how the stock is perceived. If the price is too low, the stock will appear weak; if the price is too high, the stock will be less competitive.

10. **Sell the stock.** This is the moment of truth. You're finally ready to make the stock available to the public. Now it's up to the underwriter to find a market for it.

Exempt Public Offerings

If you need to raise only a few million dollars or less, some of these steps can be simplified or eliminated. The SEC permits "exempt" public offerings of unregistered securities when (1) small amounts of capital are required and (2) the investors are considered to be "knowledgeable" about the securities being offered.

Making an exempt offering has the advantage of saving time and money while cutting back significantly on your disclosure and reporting requirements. Given the nature of the offering, though, it limits the amount of capital you can raise and generally results in lower stock prices and less owner liquidity since the shares are more difficult to trade.

The Registration Statement—Outline

Part I
▶ Type of securities offered
▶ Description of the company
  Background information
  Main products or services
  Target markets
  Competitive environment
  Patents, trademarks, licenses held
  Employees
  Distribution system
  Research and development activities
  Largest customers/key contracts
  Properties owned
▶ Financial data and audited statements
▶ Information on company officers and directors
▶ Risk factors affecting the business
▶ Terms of the underwriting agreement
▶ Advisers assisting in the IPO
▶ Past or pending legal proceedings

Part II
▶ Information on recent sales of unregistered securities
▶ Corporate documents:
  Articles of incorporation and by-laws
  Employment contracts
  Pension and stock option plans
▶ Supplemental financial data
▶ Expenses related to the offering
▶ Underwriting contract

13 | TAXING DECISIONS

From the start-up stage on, entrepreneurs need to take a vigorous approach to lowering their taxes. In growing your business you can't afford to ignore the tax implications inherent in virtually every management decision. Even in areas where taxes are the farthest thought from your mind, they can often enter into the picture.

Eroding profits and threatening assets, taxes can seem like an unbeatable foe. With planning, though, there are a number of strategies you can employ to minimize your tax burden and take the bite out of your tax bill.

STARTING OUT RIGHT

The time to begin thinking about taxes is at the very outset, when a business is just getting started. The decisions that are made during the planning phase and first year of operations are critical, carrying a weight that will be felt throughout the life of the business, increasing in importance as your business grows.

Legal Structure

One of the most important decisions is your choice of a legal structure. Having tax consequences, as well as operational ones, this choice has an impact on matters ranging from how your income and expenses are treated to the distribution of earnings and transfer of ownership.

The four types of legal structure include: sole proprietorship, partnership, corporation, and S corporation. Differing in both the ways they are established and function, each structure has its own set of tax rules to follow.

Sole Proprietorship

The simplest legal structure you can choose, a sole proprietorship is a business that is owned by just one person who is entitled to all of its profits and responsible for all of its debts. Established with a minimum of government paperwork, a sole proprietorship is considered to be an extension of its owner with no separate legal standing. In the eyes of the law, you and the business are viewed as one.

When it comes to taxes, these are some of the rules that apply to a sole proprietorship:

▶ The organizational costs to create the business cannot be recovered (amortized) since the owner is essentially the "organization"; however, start-up costs to investigate the business and get it started *can* be recovered.
▶ The business itself does not have to pay any income taxes; profits or losses are included with the owner's other income, if any, and taxed as personal income.
▶ The business has the option of using a *cash accounting method*, which counts income when it is received, or an *accrual accounting method*, which counts income when it is earned.

▶ There is no tax effect if the owner transfers money or property to or from the business.

▶ The sale or purchase of a sole proprietorship is not considered as a single transaction encompassing the entire business unit, but as several transactions pertaining to individual business assets; as such, each "transaction" must be reported separately.

Partnership

A partnership is the relationship that exists when two or more people join forces to carry on a trade or business. Contributing money, property, labor, or skill to the enterprise, each partner is entitled to share in the proceeds of the business. Each, in turn, is liable for its debts. Like a sole proprietorship, a partnership has no separate standing and isn't required to obtain a state charter to do business. However, it's advisable to have a written partnership agreement specifying the terms of the relationship and the rights and responsibilities of the partners.

When it comes to taxes, these are some of the rules that apply to a partnership:

▶ Both the organizational costs associated with putting the partnership together and the start-up costs to launch the business are recoverable; this includes legal, accounting, and consulting fees.

▶ The business itself does not have to pay income taxes although it is required to file a return for informational purposes; profits or losses are apportioned to the partners and taxed as personal income.

▶ The business has the option of using a cash or accrual accounting method unless it is a tax shelter or has a corporation as a partner; then it must use the accrual basis.

▶ Transfers of money or other property between the partners

and the business may or may not have a tax effect depending on the nature of the transfer.

▶ Ownership in a partnership is transferred through the sale or purchase of a partner's interest in the business; the selling partner reports the transaction as a capital gain or loss. When a partner leaves or joins the business, the old partnership is dissolved and a new one must be created unless the partnership agreement stipulates otherwise.

Corporation

A corporation is unique in that it has a legal standing separate from its owners. The law considers it to be an "artificial being" with the same rights and responsibilities of a person including the right to own property and enter into contracts, to sue and be sued, lend and invest money, and so on. It is the most difficult legal structure to form, since a corporation must be granted a state charter to conduct business. The owners, who are shareholders in the corporation, receive dividends based on earnings. And, unlike a sole proprietor or partner, each shareholder's liability for debts is limited only to the amount of his or her investment.

When it comes to taxes, the following rules apply:

▶ Both the organizational costs associated with creating the corporation and the start-up costs to launch it are recoverable. In addition to the legal, accounting, and consulting fees, this includes the cost of temporary directors, organizational meetings, and state incorporation fees.

▶ The business itself is required to pay income taxes. In what amounts to *double taxation*, the corporation pays a tax on the income it earns, then the owners pay another tax on the income when they receive it.

▶ The business must use the accrual accounting method unless excepted under IRS guidelines.

▶ Transfers of money or other property between shareholders and the business may or may not have a tax effect.

▶ Ownership in a corporation can be easily transferred through the sale or purchase of stock; the shareholder selling the stock reports the transaction as a capital gain or loss. The corporation's legal standing remains the same. Since a corporation is a separate entity, its continued existence is unaffected by changes in ownership, giving it the potential for "unlimited life."

S Corporation

An S corporation is a legal structure that possesses the attributes of a corporation, but is taxed as a partnership. This enables it to enjoy the benefits of a corporation while avoiding the double taxation. However, the advantage comes at a price. There are various restrictions on the number and type of shareholders an S corporation can have, on its organization, and on its stock.

When it comes to taxes, these are the rules that apply to an S corporation:

▶ Both the organizational and start-up costs are recoverable.

▶ The business itself does not have to pay income taxes; instead it passes items of income, loss, deduction, and credit through to the shareholders to be included in their personal returns.

▶ The business has the option of using a cash or accrual accounting method.

▶ Transfers of money or other property between the shareholders and the business may or may not have a tax effect.

▶ Ownership in an S corporation is more difficult to transfer than in a corporation since there are restrictions on who may be shareholder.

Financing

The method you use to finance your business also has tax consequences. Given a choice between debt and equity financing, you must not only consider the repayment and ownership issues, but the tax ones. In the case of debt, the interest paid to lenders is tax deductible; in the case of equity, the dividends paid to investors are not. Furthermore, as an owner, whether you designate money you put into the business as a loan or an investment may have an impact on your personal taxes. For example, if your business is a corporation and you lend money to it, when the money is repaid you would be taxed only on the interest you receive, not the principal. With an investment, though, any repayment you receive would likely be taxed as dividend income unless the company reports it as a "nontaxable return of capital."

Location

Another critical decision when considering tax implications is where to locate your business. The tax impact of doing business in one state can be radically different from doing business in another state. Income taxes and sales taxes are just two of the state levies that can cut into your profits. Others include: incorporation fees, property taxes, equipment taxes, the fees for licenses and permits, public utilities assessments, environmental fees, and so on. And, it's no small change; it can get to the point where a business is paying more in state and local taxes than it is in federal taxes.

Choosing a business-friendly state in which to establish your business or open up additional branches can go a long way to reducing your tax bill. It may not go far enough, though. You don't have to actually *be* in a state to be liable for its taxes; simply "doing business" in a state can be grounds for taxation.

A business is allowed to solicit customers in another state without incurring local taxes, but if its sales staff *services* the customers there then it can be liable for taxes. To avoid this you should handle customers' post-sale questions and take care of credit and collection matters from your main office. And, to play it safe, it's a good idea to make out-of-state deliveries by common carrier, rather than using your own trucks.

Accounting Methods

Your choice of an accounting method can make a difference, too. Affecting not only how you report income and expenses, but how items are treated, it's important to pick the method, or combination of methods, that best fits your needs. Under the *cash* method of accounting, income is reported in the year it is received and expenses are deducted in the year they are paid. Under the *accrual* method of accounting, income is reported when it is earned, whether or not it's been received, and expenses are deducted when you become liable for them, whether or not they've been paid.

The cash accounting method offers the advantage of letting you shift your tax obligation to the following year by postponing the receipt of income that is due. On the downside, though, you cannot deduct your expenses until they are actually paid. So, if your expenses are high, this method could end up costing you more.

The accrual method lets you deduct your expenses when they are incurred. Also, it's generally better for business planning purposes, since it more accurately matches your income and expenses to the activities that generated them. The disadvantage, of course, is having to pay taxes on income in the year it's earned even though it may be months before you receive it.

In adopting or changing your accounting method, you want to take a close look at your income and expense *patterns* before making your selection. The choice may not be up to you, though. Corporations and partnerships that have corporations as partners are required to use the accrual method. Businesses that have inventory for sale must also use the accrual method to account for their purchases and sales. However, if they want to use the cash method to report their other items of income and expense, they may, in effect combining the two methods.

Research and Development Costs

Any research costs you incur to develop or improve a product, formula, process, or invention can be recovered from your taxes. Here the decision you must make is whether to treat them as *expenses* or *capital costs*. The difference is that expenses are deducted from your current taxes, while capital costs are amortized over a period of years. Neither method is better than the other. The method you select depends on whether it's more advantageous for you to recover your costs sooner or later, in one tax year or spread out over several.

WATCHING THE BOTTOM LINE

Once you've made the initial tax decisions associated with growing a business there are other decisions to make. Relating to how you operate your business, these can have a big impact on your bottom line.

Deductible Expenses

To avoid paying more taxes than you should, your accounting system must be able to accurately track and report all deductible expenses. This entails knowing what expenses are deductible and what are not and the proper procedures for substantiating them. In the words of the Internal Revenue Service, "To be deductible a business expense must be ordinary in your business and necessary for its operation." The IRS goes on to say, "The word *ordinary* refers to an expense that is common and accepted practice in the industry. *Necessary* expenses are those that are appropriate and helpful in developing and maintaining your business."

The issue of what's "ordinary" and what's "necessry" isn't always as cut and dry as it might seem, though. So, when it comes to the handling of expense items you must make your decisions carefully and then be prepared to defend them. Among the expense items that would generally meet the government's standards for deductibility are:

- ► Accounting fees
- ► Advertising
- ► Automobile
- ► Charitable donations
- ► Consulting fees
- ► Credit reports
- ► Depreciation
- ► Entertainment
- ► Fringe benefits
- ► Gifts
- ► Insurance
- ► Interest
- ► Legal fees
- ► Licenses
- ► Maintenance
- ► Materials
- ► Postage
- ► Printing
- ► Professional memberships
- ► Publicity
- ► Rent
- ► Safe deposit box
- ► Salaries
- ► Sales commissions
- ► Stationery
- ► Supplies
- ► Taxes
- ► Trade publications
- ► Travel
- ► Utilities

Some expense categories in particular where attention to detail can result in big tax savings, include owner and employee benefits, travel and entertainment, and automobile expenses.

Owner and Employee Benefits

A good benefits program not only meets your own needs and those of workers, but is cost- and tax-effective. Offering such features as protection against loss of income, health care coverage, paid vacations and holidays, educational assistance, and so on, a benefits program isn't something you should attempt to design by yourself. To achieve your objectives and comply with government regulations, it's best to obtain the advice of a benefits planning expert.

Inasmuch as benefits can equal up to 40 percent of the average worker's salary, the decisions that you make regarding what to include in your benefits program and how to administer it must be considered from all angles. Whenever possible, two goals you should try to meet are that the benefits you provide be (1) deductible by your business and (2) nontaxable to employees.

Travel and Entertainment

Travel and entertainment expenses can be deducted as long as they are business related and conform to the tax rules currently in effect.

In the case of travel expenses, they must be incurred away from home and be ordinary and necessary in running your business. Travel expenses that would normally be deductible include the ones shown in the chart on page 176.

Entertainment expenses for meals, tickets to social, theatrical or sports events, recreational activities, and so on must also be ordinary and necessary expenditures. The two main things to keep in mind in calculating them are (1) to separate personal expenses from business ones and (2) to substantiate all deductions with adequate documentation.

For each expense item you should have a record of the kind

DEDUCTIBLE TRAVEL EXPENSES

EXPENSES	DESCRIPTION
Transportation	The cost of travel by airplane, train, or bus between your home and your business destination.
Taxi, commuter bus, and limousine	Fares for these and other types of transportation between the airport or station and your hotel, or between the hotel and your work site away from home.
Baggage and shipping	The cost of sending baggage and sample or display material between your regular and temporary work sites.
Car	The cost of operating and maintaining your car when traveling away from home on business. You may deduct actual expenses or the standard mileage rate, including business-related tolls and parking. If you lease a car while away from home on business, you can deduct business-related expenses only.
Lodging	The cost of lodging if your business trip is overnight or long enough to require you to get substantial sleep or rest to properly perform your duties.
Meals	The cost of meals only if your business trip is overnight or long enough to require you to stop to get substantial sleep or rest. Includes amounts spent for food, beverages, taxes, and related tips.
Cleaning	Cleaning and laundry expenses while away from home overnight.
Telephone	The cost of business calls while on your business trip, including business communication by fax machine or other communication devices.
Tips	Tips you pay for any expenses in this chart.
Other	Other similar and necessary expenses related to your business travel, such as public stenographer's fees and computer rental fees.

of expense, the amount, when and where it occurred, and its business purpose. The IRS advises keeping the proof you need in an "account book, diary, statement of expenses, or similar record" along with adequate documentary evidence, such as receipts, cancelled checks, or bills.

Automobile Expense

The costs associated with using automobiles or trucks in your business can also be deducted. This includes such expenses as gasoline, oil, maintenance and repairs, insurance, depreciation, interest on car payments, taxes, license fees, parking charges, and tolls. You can calculate the amount of your deduction by either (1) keeping an actual record of all expenses or (2) multiplying the number of yearly miles driven times the government's standard mileage rate.

It's important to note that if a vehicle is used for both business and personal use, the costs arising from the personal use are not deductible. You can claim only the business portion. Thus, if a car is driven a total of 20,000 miles in a year and 12,000 miles are for business and 8,000 miles are for personal use, only 60 percent (12,000/20,000) of the total operating expenses are deductible.

In deciding which method to use, you should try calculating your automobile expenses both ways. Then use the method that is most advantageous.

Earnings Distribution

How and when you elect to distribute accumulated earnings is another decision that carries tax consequences. This is especially true for corporations. The choices—to retain the earnings in the business, distribute them as salaries, or pay them out as dividends—need to be evaluated with an eye toward reducing your tax liability. Higher salaries increase the recipients' tax burden and could be perceived as excessive by shareholders. Dividends, on the other hand, aren't a deductible business expense. And, simply keeping the earnings in your business could trigger an *accumulated earnings tax* if the IRS believes the business has cash reserves beyond its reasonable needs.

Getting around these problems can take some doing. In the last case—allowing the earnings to accumulate—one way is to show that you are holding the funds for a legitimate purpose, such as an upcoming project or planned expansion.

Depreciation

As your business expands and acquires more property you need to keep a close watch on depreciation—the property's loss in value over its lifetime. Much of this loss can be recovered either by claiming it as a tax deduction the first year that you have the property or by taking deductions over a specified period of years. To make the right decisions, you must be familiar with the IRS rules governing the types of property that can be depreciated and the allowable recovery period for each property class (automobiles, equipment, office furniture, buildings, patents, and copyrights, etc.). There are also separate rules pertaining to the percentage of the loss that is recoverable each year. Maintaining good accounting records is critical especially if you have numerous items to depreciate or the depreciation is spread over a long period of time.

Inventory Valuation

If you're in a business where it's necessary to keep inventory on hand—merchandise, raw materials, component parts, work in process, finished products—you must decide on the method you want to use to determine the value of that inventory. This decision is important because inventory value is a major factor in calculating your taxable income.

There are three methods to choose from: (1) specific identification, (2) FIFO, and (3) LIFO. These are defined as follows:

Specific identification. This method matches each inventory item with its cost of acquisition and other allocable costs, such as labor and transportation.

FIFO. This method doesn't match specific inventory items to specific costs. Instead, it assumes that the items you purchased or produced *first* during the year were sold first ("first in, first out"). Thus the value of the items on hand at the end of the year is set at the cost of your most recent acquisitions.

LIFO. This method is similar to FIFO except it assumes that the items you purchased or produced *last* during the year were sold first ("last in, first out"). As such, the value of the items on hand at the end of the year is set at the cost of your oldest acquisitions.

The specific identification method is the most accurate, but it is also the most time-consuming and it may not result in the greatest tax savings. In times of inflation, when prices are rising, the LIFO method is best since it lowers the value of the inventory while raising the cost of goods sold, thus reducing your income tax liability. Conversely, when prices are falling, the FIFO method is best.

Sale of Assets

Selling assets used in your business also calls for tax strategy. If the transaction is going to result in a gain, one way you can defer your tax liability is to structure the payment in *install-ments,* rather than one lump sum. This enables you to spread out the gain over more than one year and/or to recognize it in a year when your tax rate is lower. Another technique you should consider is *exchanging,* rather than selling, the asset. This lets you postpone the gain until the time that you sell the exchanged property. In using this method, though, the assets being exchanged must be of "like-kind," or similar in nature. If money or other property (collectively called the "boot") is included in the exchange, the amount of gain on that is taxable in the year it's received.

Tax Credits

In operating your business it's also important to be aware of the tax credits you may be eligible to receive. These are provided by the government as a way of encouraging businesses to pursue certain objectives or to accommodate disadvantaged groups. For example, tax credits available to businesses include the

- ▶ **Disabled Access Credit.** For businesses that pay or incur expenses to provide access to persons with disabilities.
- ▶ **Job Credit.** For businesses that hire persons from targeted groups that have a particularly high unemployment rate or special employment needs.
- ▶ **Research Credit.** For businesses that increase the amounts they spend on research and experimental activities.

PERSONAL MATTERS

Many of the decisions that you make will have a personal tax effect as well as a business one, especially those that pertain to your individual income taxes and the disposition of assets. In keeping with your goals of lowering your taxes and preserving assets, two things you should become familiar with are *income shifting* and *estate planning*.

Income Shifting

Income shifting is a tax-planning method that enables you to reduce your taxes by shifting income to family members, such as school-aged children or retired parents who are in lower tax brackets. This can be done by transferring stocks, bonds, or other income-generating assets to them or by employing them in your business and paying them a wage. The added advantage of employing family members is that the wage paid to them can be claimed as a deductible business expense.

In using these techniques, though, you want to make sure that the tax reductions to be gained from the income shift exceed any tax increases or penalties that occur. For example, in hiring children you could lose your right to claim them as dependents, and employed parents could have their social security benefits reduced.

Furthermore, to comply with the law, the family members must actually perform work for the business. It's not enough to just put them on the payroll. They must earn their pay.

Estate Planning

No one relishes the idea of facing one's own mortality, but estate planning is a necessary part of growing a business. To protect what you've worked to build, it's important to develop a plan that will keep your assets from being eroded by estate and income taxes and ensure that they are distributed according to your wishes.

Estate planning is a task that calls for the services of a good tax lawyer, and can mean the difference between keeping your business intact or breaking it up; between providing loved ones with financial security or subjecting them to tax liabilities. To accomplish your intended purpose, it must be an ongoing process. You should review your plan periodically and modify it, as needed, to reflect any changes that have taken place in your business or family. In the event that you retire or sell the business or a birth, death, or marriage occurs, these factors should be incorporated into the plan along with any changes in the health or financial status of your intended beneficiaries; so should any changes in the tax laws.

With the right planning and proper use of such tax-saving alternatives as the marital deduction, life insurance, cash gifts throughout your lifetime, and trusts, you can preserve the value of your estate and achieve your objectives.

14 | MONITORING PERFORMANCE

To stop problems before they begin and identify any areas that need improvement, it's important to monitor your business's performance on a regular basis. As your business grows, there's no escaping the need to continually assess where it is and where it's going.

The best way to keep your business on track and moving in the right direction is to establish guidelines that can be used to measure its progress. These guidelines will tell you how your business is doing in key areas, and should be both quantitative and qualitative in nature. *Quantitative guidelines* are objective measurements based on verifiable facts. *Qualitative guidelines* are subjective measurements based on observation and judgment.

QUANTITATIVE GUIDELINES

Quantitative guidelines provide a means of evaluating the performance of your business in terms of its ability to meet financial goals and operate within budget constraints. Relying on past and current financial data, they can help you to determine how profitable the business is and whether or not its resources are being put to the best use.

Ratio Analysis

One of the most effective tools you can use to evaluate your financial performance is *ratio analysis*. This entails studying the relationships (expressed as ratios) that exist among the figures in your financial statements—the income statement and the balance sheet. The resultant information can then be used to compare (1) past and present performance and (2) business performance with industry norms.

The most frequently used ratios fall into these four categories:

- Liquidity ratios
- Operating ratios
- Profitability ratios
- Leverage ratios

Liquidity ratios

These measure your business's ability to meet its short-term financial obligations and to convert assets into cash. The two most widely known ratios in this group are the *current ratio* and the *acid-test ratio* (also called the "quick ratio").

Current ratio. Comparing your current assets to your current liabilities, this ratio measures the ability of your business to pay its debts in the year ahead. The measurement that creditors generally look at first, it's calculated as follows:

$$\text{Current ratio} = \frac{\text{Current assets}}{\text{Current liabilities}}$$

Although circumstances can vary, normally a minimum ratio of 2 to 1 is expected, meaning the business has two dollars in current assets for each dollar of current liabilities.

Acid-test ratio. This ratio is like the current ratio except that it excludes inventory, which can be difficult to sell, from the asset total. Taking into consideration only your most "liquid" assets—cash, marketable securities, and accounts receivable— you calculate it as follows:

$$\text{Acid-test ratio} = \frac{\text{Cash} + \text{marketable securities} + \text{accounts receivable}}{\text{Current liabilities}}$$

In this case a ratio of 1 to 1 is generally considered acceptable.

Profitability ratios

These measure your business's ability to achieve desired profit levels and use its assets effectively. The ratios that investors are usually most interested in include your *net profit on sales, return on investment (ROI), return on equity (ROE), and earnings per share* ratios:

Net profit on sales. Comparing your net profit to net sales, this ratio measures the ability of your business to turn a profit on the sales it makes. The profit percentage on each dollar of sales, it's calculated as follows:

$$\text{Net profit on sales} = \frac{\text{Net profit}}{\text{Net sales}}$$

There's no set percentage that's considered acceptable since each industry is different, but the higher the percentage, the greater your sales efficiency.

Return on investment. This ratio also looks at your net profit, but here, it is compared to your total assets to determine if they are generating sufficient income. The profit percentage for each dollar of investment, it's calculated as follows:

$$\text{Return on investment} = \frac{\text{Net profit}}{\text{Total assets}}$$

Again there's no set percentage that's considered acceptable; but the higher the percentage, the better your assets are being utilized.

Return on equity. Narrowing the focus from the return on total assets to the return on shareholders' equity, this ratio is of particular importance to investors. To show them whether the rate of return justifies the risk of investing in your business, calculate as follows:

$$\text{Return on equity} = \frac{\text{Net profit}}{\text{Shareholders' equity}}$$

The higher the percentage, the better the rate of return, making investors more willing to accept the risk.

Earnings per share. Another ratio investors are concerned with, this shows the distribution of earnings based on the number of shares of stock that are outstanding. The measure of the business's profitability in terms of the money available to investors, it is calculated as shown:

$$\text{Earnings per share} = \frac{\text{Net income}}{\text{Number of shares outstanding}}$$

The higher the earnings per share, the greater the potential payoff to investors and the more desirable the investment is considered to be.

Operating ratios.

These measure your business's ability to conduct its ongoing activities and carry out its objectives in a cost-effective manner. Among the ratios to watch are your *average collection period* and *inventory turnover.*

Average collection period. Used to determine if customers are paying their bills when they should, this ratio focuses on your accounts receivable procedures. Showing the average number of days needed to collect receivables, it's calculated like this:

$$\text{Average collection period} = \frac{\text{Average receivables} \times 365}{\text{Net credit sales}}$$

The collection period that's acceptable depends on your credit terms and what's typical for your industry. As a rule of thumb, though, it shouldn't exceed one and one-third times your credit terms ($1\frac{1}{3} \times 30$ days $= 40$ days).

Inventory turnover. This ratio is used to assess how quickly your business is able to sell its inventory. The number of times the inventory is sold out, or "turned over," during the year, it is calculated as follows:

$$\text{Inventory turnover} = \frac{\text{Cost of goods sold}}{\text{Average inventory}}$$

The higher your turnover rate, the faster you're moving the goods and making way for more inventory. This not only adds to your sales volume, but reduces your risk of getting stuck with obsolete, unsalable inventory due to changes in customer tastes or technology.

Leverage ratios

These measure your business's ability to service its long-term debt and balance the needs of creditors and investors. Showing the amount of "leverage" between borrowed funds and equity capital, the key ratios include your *debt to assets* and *debt to equity* ratios.

Debt to assets. This ratio shows the extent to which borrowed funds have been used to finance the business. Comparing your debt load to your total assets, it's calculated like this:

$$\text{Debt to assets} = \frac{\text{Total debt}}{\text{Total assets}}$$

Another one of the figures creditors look at closely, it tells the percentage of your assets that are already subject to creditors' claims. The lower the percentage, the more assets available to be used as loan collateral.

Debt to equity. This ratio looks at the level of debt, too. A comparison of the funds provided by creditors with those provided by investors, it's calculated as follows:

$$\text{Debt to equity} = \frac{\text{Total debt}}{\text{Total equity}}$$

A ratio of 1 to 1 or better is generally recommended, meaning that for each dollar of borrowed funds, there is one dollar of invested funds.

For help in analyzing your financial ratios and to see how your business stacks up against others in its field there are a number of reference books that you can use. Two of the most comprehensive ones are Robert Morris Associates' *Annual Statement*

Studies and Dun & Bradstreet's *Industry Norms & Key Business Ratios.* Both books are updated each year and provide financial benchmarks for businesses in hundreds of industries.

Budgets

Another important monitoring tool is your budget. Consisting of formal statements about your business's projected revenues, expenses, and profits, your budget should be viewed as both a *planning* and a *control* device. By setting forth what you hope to accomplish and the resources available to do it, a budget provides a realistic framework for the planning process to take place. And by stating specific output/input objectives—resources expended/revenues earned—the budget serves a control function, telling you whether or not financial targets are being met.

Although referred to in the singular, a budget is actually a compilation of three budgets: an operating budget; a cash budget; a capital budget.

Operating budget. This shows the amount of money, based on projected revenues, that will be available to carry out your business's ongoing operations, covering labor, materials, and overhead expenses.

Cash budget. This shows your projected revenues and expenses over a given period (a month, quarter, year), providing cash flow data that can be used in planning payments and purchases and making investment and borrowing decisions.

Capital budget. This shows anticipated major purchases of equipment, property, buildings, and other capital investments that will serve your business over a number of years.

CASH BUDGET
For Year Ending December 31, 199X

BEGINNING CASH BALANCE, January 1, 199X   _____

CASH RECEIPTS (Estimated)

   Cash sales   _____

   Collections on accounts receivable   _____

   Collections on all other receivables   _____

   Interest   _____

   Dividends   _____

   Sale of assets   _____

   Capital stock issued   _____

   Bonds issued   _____

   Bank loans   _____

   Other money borrowed   _____

     Total estimated cash receipts   _____

CASH DISBURSEMENTS (Estimated)

   Cash purchases   _____

   Payments on accounts payable   _____

   Bank loan payments   _____

   Bond payments   _____

   Mortgage payments   _____

   Retirement of other debt   _____

   Retirement of capital stock   _____

   Interest   _____

   Taxes   _____

   Dividends paid   _____

   Fixed asset expenditures   _____

   Direct labor expenses   _____

   Selling expenses   _____

   Manufacturing expenses   _____

   All other expenditures   _____

     Total estimated cash disbursements   _____

ENDING CASH BALANCE (Estimated),   _____
December 31, 199X

These budgets provide a vital link in the planning and implementation process, allocating resources where they will do the most good and enabling you to measure your performance by comparing budget projections with actual results. Using a cash budget worksheet similar to the one on page 190 will help to ensure that you have adequate funds on hand when you need them and that your money is being put to the best use.

Showing the projected cash flows for the year, the budget pinpoints the various sources and uses of funds during the coming months. Since the figures are only projections, though, it's important to review them throughout the year, comparing them to the actual results.

QUALITATIVE GUIDELINES

Qualitative guidelines provide a means of evaluating the nonfinancial side of your business in terms of the human factors that enable it to accomplish its objectives. Utilizing such tools as observation, experience, and feedback, they can enable you to rate the effectiveness of your management team and to determine how well critical business functions are being carried out.

Management by Objectives

A method of evaluating worker performance that has been well received by employees and employers alike is *management by objectives* (MBO). In an effort to quantify the essentially qualitative task of rating employees' achievement levels, it defines what's expected in advance, setting specific objectives for each employee. The goals, which are mutually agreed upon by the worker and the worker's boss, are then checked at periodic intervals to determine if progress is being made toward reaching them. This way, rather than having to subjectively assess whether or not the worker is performing well, you have *concrete* proof. And the worker does, too. As a result, it's easier to gauge if the needs of the business are being met. Also, employees know what they have to do to suceed and, by helping to set the goals, feel a greater commitment to them.

As shown here, the MBO evaluation method works like this:

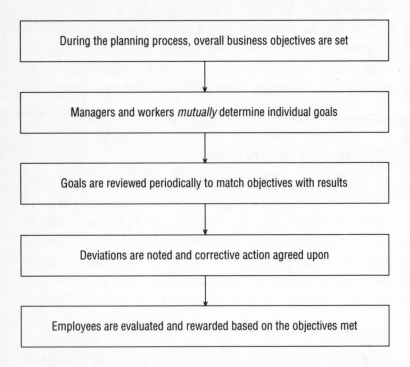

During the planning process, overall business objectives are set

Managers and workers *mutually* determine individual goals

Goals are reviewed periodically to match objectives with results

Deviations are noted and corrective action agreed upon

Employees are evaluated and rewarded based on the objectives met

Once the last step is completed the cycle repeats itself. New objectives are set and the employee evaluation process begins again.

360-Degree Evaluation

This evaluation method rates employees from a different perspective—how they are seen by their superiors, peers, and subordinates. Based on the assumption that "no man is an island," it looks beyond the individual's ability to achieve his or her own objectives and determines how the person is at helping others to achieve *their* objectives. Relying on coworker feedback, it evaluates the employee's ability to function as a team player, assessing such skills and values as cooperation, communication, reliability, innovation, and integrity.

Providing insights that would otherwise be hard to come by, a 360-degree evaluation doesn't always tell people what they want to hear; but it tells them what they *need* to hear. Though sometimes tough to swallow, the inputs gained in this way can have a profoundly beneficial impact on employees, showing them which areas need to be improved and enhancing their work relationships.

Management Audit

Rather than looking at individual workers, a *management audit* looks at your business as a whole, evaluating your people, policies and procedures, strengths and weaknesses to determine your organizational effectiveness. Much the way a financial audit examines your financial resources and how they're being utilized, this examines your human resources and their utilization.

Some of the areas most frequently evaluated in a management audit include:

• Planning procedures and guidelines
• Organization structure
• Management abilities and effectiveness
• Marketing strategies
• Research and development activities
• Production methods and efficiency

- Competitiveness
- Employment practices and compensation
- Compliance with applicable laws
- Customer relations

In conducting a management audit, you can either have your own personnel do it or use an outside consultant. In recent years an increasing number of public accounting firms have branched out into this area as well, adding management audits to the growing array of services they provide. Using inside personnel is generally faster and cheaper, but not all staffs are capable of performing a management audit and the findings may not be as objective as they should be. Going outside gets around those problems, but has its own drawbacks, including auditors who may not be familiar with your type of business and possible leaks of proprietary information.

CRITICAL AREAS TO WATCH

In monitoring your business performance it's important to see how the various guidelines being utilized apply to these critical areas:

1. Profitability	Are profit targets being met or exceeded?
2. Asset usage	Are assets being used in a way that will result in the greatest economic benefit?
3. Productivity	Are productivity levels where they should be?

4. Marketing strategy   Are the right target markets being served in the most efficient way possible?

5. Leadership   Are managers providing the guidance and support workers need to perform their jobs?

6. Workforce capability   Are workers willing and able to carry out their respective tasks?

7. Customer relations   Are customers' needs being met as well as they can be?

8. Creativity   Are new ideas and strategies welcomed and encouraged?

9. Integrity   Are all people associated with the business behaving in an ethical manner?

15 | GETTING OUTSIDE HELP

Contrary to what most people think, the main reason businesses fail isn't because of a lack of money. Rather, it's because owners and managers lack the knowledge, experience, or simply the time needed to carry out the various tasks associated with running their businesses. This isn't a problem for small businesses alone, but for larger ones as well, especially when they enter a new field or achieve rapid growth in a short period. The increased demands of an expanded customer base, work force, or production-distribution system can easily tax the abilities of even the most competent management team.

Fortunately, there are outside services and specialists you can turn to for help when you need it. Whatever you need—assistance in planning, obtaining capital, recruiting and training workers, marketing, dealing with tax and legal matters, or virtually any other area—help is available—often at little or no cost to you.

To get the assistance you need, while keeping your fixed payroll expenses down, it's important to know about the outside help you can get from government, business, association, and academic sources.

GOVERNMENT SOURCES

One of the first places you should look for help in growing your business is the United States government—at the federal, state, or local level. Of the services available to you, you'll find that, in addition to the quality and quantity, many of them are provided free of charge or for only a nominal fee.

Department of Commerce

The Department of Commerce's (DOC) primary objective is to support and promote the concerns of American businesses. Through its specialists, programs, publications, and unsurpassed economic data base, it can provide the information and assistance businesses need to compete effectively both in the United States and abroad. For help in marketing research, international trade, selling to the government, job training, developing new technologies, or other business-related areas, you should take advantage of the services available to you through the DOC.

Some of the DOC's publications and reports most helpful to growing businesses include the:

Bureau of Economic Analysis Reports, providing information on the current state of the U.S. economy and on exports and imports.

Census Bureau Statistical Profiles, providing information on the population (age, income, family status, occupation, education, and housing) and trends related to consumer and government spending.

Commerce Business Daily, providing information on civilian and military procurement needs and federal contract awards; published daily, it is available by subscription from the Government Printing Office.

Survey of Current Business, providing information updates on the nation's economy and business outputs.

To find out which branch office is closest to you, obtain publications, or talk to a specialist, contact the Department of Commerce, Washington, D.C. 20230.

Department of Labor

As your business grows, the information available from the Department of Labor (DOL) will become increasingly important to you. The Department of Labor can provide you with data pertaining to economic growth, the labor force, worker productivity, and the cost of living. In addition to this, it can answer your questions on such labor issues as minimum wages and overtime pay, unemployment insurance, workers' compensation, nondiscrimination laws, occupational safety and health, training programs, pension planning, and many others.

The DOL has various programs designed to assist employers who hire disadvantaged workers or provide education and job training. These can help you to reduce your payroll and training expenses.

To obtain the latest labor information or find out about incentive or assistance programs your business may be eligible to participate in, contact the Department of Labor, Washington, D.C. 20210.

Economic Development Offices

Many local governments maintain economic development offices to assist the businesses within their communities. Their goals are to promote local businesses and, in so doing, create jobs for area residents and generate municipal tax revenues. If your community has an economic development office, this can be a valuable resource for you, providing information on the local economy, construction activity, population and labor force, wages and salaries, consumer spending, public services, business and zoning regulations, and so on.

Export-Import Bank

The Export-Import Bank (EXIMBANK) is an independent government agency that assists businesses in obtaining export financing and credit insurance to protect themselves against foreign debtor defaults. The agency's primary form of business assistance is its *Working Capital Guarantee Program*, which guarantees up to 90 percent of the value of a commercial loan to your business for the purpose of meeting your pre-export working capital needs. The kinds of loans that would come under the "working capital" category include money borrowed to purchase inventory, develop export marketing programs, take foreign marketing trips, or participate in trade fairs.

For more information on the assistance available through EXIMBANK, contact the Export-Import Bank, Washington, D.C. 20571.

Federal Trade Commission

The Federal Trade Commission is the agency charged with regulating businesses to ensure that they don't engage in unfair methods of competition, false advertising, or deceptive pricing, packaging, or labeling practices. Though its main function is to protect the public, the FTC spends much of its time assisting and educating businesses to be aware of what they must do to comply with the law. Thus, if you have questions about the legality of a proposed business strategy or an area that comes under the FTC's jurisdiction, it would be wise to consult with it. For example, making health claims about a food product or using the terms "light" or "low-fat" are actions that would be looked at by the FTC. Special offers, advertising directed at children or the elderly, and franchise operations are also regulated by the FTC.

To obtain the Federal Trade Commission's current guidelines or get more information on how they apply to your business, contact the Federal Trade Commission, Washington, D.C. 20580.

Government Printing Office

Another resource that shouldn't be overlooked is the Government Printing Office. The GPO is responsible for the publication, distribution, and sale of government documents, reports, books, and pamphlets on a variety of subjects, including many related to business. These publications, which usually are available for a nominal price, can be obtained from local Government Printing Office bookstores or from the GPO's headquarters.

To find out if a GPO bookstore is in your area, obtain a catalogue of publications, or purchase specific titles, write directly to the U.S. Government Printing Office, Superintendent of Documents, Washington, D.C. 20402.

Internal Revenue Service

The Internal Revenue Service can provide you with the latest information pertaining to your federal income taxes. In addition to maintaining local offices staffed with tax specialists, the IRS publishes numerous guides and circulars covering all aspects of business taxation, from deductibles and depreciation to retirement accounts and withholding. You may even find that the information available from the IRS *saves* you money by identifying allowable deductions or helping you to avoid fines or penalties.

One particularly helpful publication from the IRS is its annual *Tax Guide for Small Business*. Available free of charge, this approximately 200-page guide answers a broad range of business questions. A list of other IRS publications that may be of help to you is included at the end of this chapter.

International Trade Administration

The International Trade Administration (ITA) was established by the Department of Commerce to provide information and counseling to American businesses involved in foreign trade. The ITA can assist you in gaining access to foreign markets, finding agents and distributors, overseas buyers or licensees, conducting marketing research, obtaining financial aid, and so on. With offices located throughout the United States and Puerto Rico, the ITA offers individual counseling on a local basis, or businesses can contact ITA trade specialists at the organization's headquarters in Washington, D.C.

Some of the ITA services and programs that can make it easier for you to do business overseas include its

Agent/Distributor Service. The ITA will conduct a customized search for qualified foreign representatives, identifying up to six prospects who have an interest in representing your business.

Comparison Shopping Service. ITA staff will perform on-the-spot research to determine the market potential for your product offering in foreign countries, examining such factors as estimated sales, comparable products, distribution channels, pricing, consumer characteristics, etc.

Foreign Buyer Program. The ITA sponsors trade shows throughout the United States, where you can meet qualified foreign buyers for your products or services.

Trade Opportunities Program. The ITA maintains an electronic data base containing sales leads of overseas firms interested in representing or buying specific products.

Matchmaker Program. The ITA sponsors matchmaker events in which delegates of participating American businesses travel overseas to meet with potential licensees or joint-venture partners.

Along with this, the ITA offers businesses another resource, its *country desk* operation, which monitors worldwide economic trends. Country desk officers based at ITA headquarters track individual countries, maintaining up-to-date files on their regulations, tariffs, business practices, economic factors, growth potential, and more. Businesses wishing to make use of this information can talk to desk officers or obtain customized reports on specific countries.

To find out more about the services available through the ITA, contact the International Trade Administration, Washington, D.C. 20230.

Public Libraries

The United States has one of the best public library systems in the world, providing access to information on practically any business topic you're likely to encounter. In addition to the books available, there are magazines, newspapers, government publications, maps, charts, and audiovisual materials you can use. Many libraries now provide computer access to electronic databases, as well. Whether you want to find out more about your competition, follow the latest economic and social trends, or learn about new technologies or business methods, the public library can help.

To locate the libraries in your area, check the county or city government listings in the phone book. State college and university libraries are open to the public, too, and often have excellent research facilities.

Small Business Administration

The Small Business Administration (SBA) is committed to helping small businesses in numerous ways, providing assistance in

▶ Starting a business
▶ Developing markets
▶ Improving management skills
▶ Obtaining financing
▶ Procuring government contracts

This assistance is made available to businesses at nominal fees or free of charge through SBA-sponsored workshops and seminars, individual counseling, and publications. Making it easy for businesses to utilize its services, the SBA maintains more than 100 local offices nationwide.

With the help of Service Corps of Retired Executives (SCORE) and Active Corps of Executives (ACE) volunteers, the SBA offers such services as:

Management and Marketing Assistance. The SBA provides ongoing training and advice designed to help businesses develop and better serve their markets. In-depth counseling, seminars, and publications offer guidance in such areas as planning, business communications, personnel, product development, market research, advertising, and sales.

Financial Assistance. The SBA provides direct and indirect loans to businesses to help finance the acquisition of facilities, equipment, and supplies or to meet federal environmental and safety standards. There are also special loan programs available to assist veterans, the handicapped, women, and minorities.

Procurement Assistance. The SBA is actively involved in helping small businesses obtain government contracts and subcontracting opportunities with larger companies working on government projects. Toward this end, it maintains the *Procurement Automated Source System* (PASS), a computerized referral system cataloguing the interests and capabilities of businesses seeking work as government contractors or subcontractors.

For more information on the services provided by the SBA, contact the field office for your region, or the Small Business Administration, Washington, D.C. 20416. At the end of this chapter you'll find a list of SBA publications and the addresses of area field offices.

Small Business Development Centers

Utilizing a combination of public and private sector resources, small business development centers (SBDCs) across the United States provide entrepreneurs with one-on-one counseling, technical assistance, and training. Usually operated by colleges or universities, SBDCs can help you to develop or update your business plan, research your market, find out about government programs, network with other businesses, train your workers, prepare financial statements, and so on. Along with their own in-house consultants, SBDCs have access to outside experts in accounting, finance, law, marketing, and other areas, who can assist you in running your business more productively.

Designed to provide small businesses with the information and services they need to grow and prosper, SBDCs work with entrepreneurs on an ongoing basis throughout each stage of business development. Private and group counseling sessions are offered at no charge to clients. Seminars and special training are available for a nominal fee.

To find out if there's an SBDC in your area, contact the lead center for your state (listed at the end of this chapter).

BUSINESS SOURCES

These are some of the business and professional sources of help you can draw on when necessary:

- Accountants
- Advertising agencies
- Attorneys
- Bankers
- Collection agencies
- Computer specialists
- Credit reporting services
- Factoring services
- Graphic designers
- Insurance agents
- Management consultants
- Marketing specialists
- Public relations firms
- Temporary help services

Accountants

The services of an outside accountant can be invaluable in helping you to keep your financial records in order and make money-management decisions. Besides setting up an accounting system that's appropriate for your business, an accountant can:

▶ Prepare and interpret financial statements
▶ Help you to obtain financing
▶ Coordinate billing and payment procedures
▶ Advise on tax matters
▶ Evaluate investment opportunities

Even if you have a finance background or in-house accounting personnel, you may still need outside help on occasion. The two most likely times are when it's necessary to (1) make a financial decision beyond your area of expertise or (2) perform an independent audit of your business.

The best way to find a good accountant or accounting firm is to ask someone you know—a business associate, your attorney or banker—to recommend one. Or you can use the referral services of one of the state or national accounting associations.

Advertising Agencies

An advertising agency can make it easier to reach your target market by helping you to define your business image and communicate with potential customers. For example, an advertising agency can:

▶ Conduct marketing research
▶ Create promotional materials
▶ Determine the best media to use
▶ Monitor customer satisfaction levels

The types of advertising agencies available run the gamut from small *boutiques* that focus on the creative work of producing ads (the words and visuals) to *full-service agencies* that do everything from developing a campaign to creating the ads, obtaining media placements, and tracking the results. Some agencies specialize in helping small businesses or in promoting specific products or industries. The standard agency fee is a 15 percent commission on the cost of buying print space or air time in the media. There are also various production charges for creating the ads themselves.

To find an advertising agency that meets your needs, look in the *Standard Directory of Advertising Agencies,* a reference work carried by many public libraries, or check the *Yellow Pages.*

Attorneys
As an entrepreneur, one of the most important moves you can make is to find a good attorney. From the start-up stage on, an attorney can help your business to grow, working on your behalf to:

▶ Assist you in choosing the right legal form
▶ Negotiate agreements and draw up contracts
▶ Prepare and file government documents
▶ Secure and protect trademarks, copyrights, or patents
▶ Provide ongoing legal advice
▶ Represent you in court proceedings
▶ Oversee tax and pension planning
▶ Assist in business restructuring

To find an attorney, talk to your accountant or banker or to business associates. You can also contact your state's bar association.

Bankers

Lending money is only one of the ways your banker can help you. Bankers, as a rule, are plugged into the latest financial news, and your banker should be able to provide you with information on consumer spending patterns, investment levels, interest rates, economic trends, business developments, and so on. Your banker can also assist you in setting up your payroll, transferring funds, preparing financial reports and loan documents, obtaining letters of credit, and other money matters.

To make the most of your banking relationship, let your banker know that you value his or her expertise and want to be able to utilize it in growing your business. Not all bankers—and banks—are geared to the needs of business owners, though, and if your banker isn't willing or able to assist you, then switch to another bank that is.

Collection Agencies

No matter how good your accounts receivable system is, from time to time you're bound to have customers who don't pay their bills. When this happens, rather than dunning the customer month after month or charging off the bill, after a reasonable length of time it makes sense to turn the account over to a collection agency. The general practice in this situation is for the agency to attempt to collect the past due amount, retaining from 15 to 50 percent of the proceeds based on the size of the debt.

To locate a collection agency that can assist you, ask your accountant or banker to recommend one. Or check the *Yellow Pages* of the telephone directory.

Computer Specialists

When it comes to utilizing computers in your business, a computer specialist can save you time, money, and aggravation.

According to numerous surveys, many businesses don't know what computer equipment and software are best for them, or how to use it once they've got it.

A computer specialist can help you to get your money's worth by:

▶ Determining which software packages meet your needs
▶ Creating customized programs for you
▶ Selecting and installing equipment
▶ Taking care of service and repairs
▶ Providing computer training

To find computer specialists who can assist you in making the right decisions and keep your computer system running smoothly, check the *Yellow Pages* of your telephone directory or seek personal referrals from satisfied business associates.

Credit Reporting Services

If you allow your customers to buy on credit, the use of a credit reporting service can reduce your losses from bad debts. This is especially important if you sell high-ticket items or much of your work is performed in advance of payment.

A credit reporting service can provide you with customers'

▶ Credit histories   ▶ Driver's license records
▶ Address histories   ▶ Vehicle registration data
▶ Court records

Your banker or accountant should be able to recommend a good credit reporting service. Or check the *Yellow Pages*.

Factoring Services

Factoring services offer an important service to business—access to immediate cash—enabling you to convert your accounts receivable into dollars. An alternative to borrowing that provides financing when it's needed, factors generally pay 65 to 80 percent of the face value of the amounts owed, collecting on the accounts as they come due. Though particularly helpful to cash-strapped small businesses, factors are frequently used by larger retailers and other businesses, as well, to obtain money to replenish inventories during peak buying seasons.

To find out more about factoring services or to locate one in your area, talk to your accountant, who can explain the pros and cons of using one.

Graphic Designers

To make your promotional materials look their best you may want to have a graphic designer create the original art work. A graphic designer can help your business project the right image by designing:

▶ A logotype or identification symbol
▶ Business cards, stationery, and brochures
▶ Newsletters, manuals, and annual reports
▶ Advertising layouts
▶ Signs and packaging

Graphic designers can be especially helpful if you are doing your own advertising, rather than using an agency, by providing professional advice and services on a per project basis.

You can choose a graphic designer whose work you admire elsewhere, or call several and ask to see their portfolios so that you can gauge the quality and style of their work.

Insurance Agents

An insurance agent can help you to safeguard your business by assessing the various risks it faces and providing you with the appropriate insurance coverage. A good agent should also be able to assist you in setting up a risk-management program to reduce or eliminate risks through improved safety methods or employee training.

The best way to find an insurance agent familiar with the needs of your business is to check with others in your field or one of the trade association for your industry. In selecting an agent, it's a good idea to talk to more than one so that you can compare the coverage and costs of the insurance plans offered. Given the importance of adequately protecting your business, you can't be too careful in deciding which agent to use.

Management Consultants

Management consultants can help businesses to function more productively by streamlining operations, improving employee communications, and helping to create positive work environments. In addition to the management skills they possess, one of the main assets consultants can bring to a business is objectivity. Without preconceived ideas of how your business should be run or the need to protect their own turf, they can work with you to find the best ways to set up your organization and manage and motivate employees. Though often called in to solve problems and turn around ailing businesses, the best time to use a management consultant is *before* a problem exists or when you're embarking on something new—starting or expanding your business, entering a different field, and so on.

To find a management consultant with the skills and experience you need, check with business associates for their recommendations or look in a consulting directory. You can also contact the Institute of Management Consultants, 19 West 44th Street, New York, NY 10036.

Marketing Specialists

A marketing specialist can help you to identify your target market and put together the best strategy for getting your products or services into the marketplace. Assisting in such areas as product development, pricing, distribution, and promotion, marketing specialists can also help by:

▶ Researching your market
▶ Identifying customer needs to fill
▶ Suggesting ways to develop or modify products
▶ Determining what prices you should charge
▶ Setting up distribution arrangements
▶ Advising which media to use

To find a marketing specialist who can give you a competitive edge, check with business associates or look in a consulting directory. You can also contact the American Marketing Association, 222 South Riverside Plaza, Chicago, IL 60606.

Public Relations Firms

A public relations firm can be instrumental in obtaining publicity for your business and drawing attention to your products or services. Not just for Big Business, public relations firms can help smaller businesses to grow by getting them free media exposure and increasing their name recognition.

Among the services a public relations firm can perform are:

▶ Writing and distributing news releases
▶ Preparing media information kits
▶ Writing speeches and presentations
▶ Arranging press interviews
▶ Coaching on speaking techniques
▶ Advising on wardrobe and grooming matters
▶ Coordinating special events

To find a public relations firm that can keep your name in the public eye, look in *O'Dwyer's Directory of Public Relations Firms* in your library's reference section.

Temporary Help Services

Temporary help services are playing an increasingly important role in helping American businesses to meet their personnel needs. In addition to providing qualified secretaries, receptionists, and general office workers on a moment's notice, temporary help services can provide virtually any other worker you need—engineers, computer programmers, sales and marketing professionals, accountants, attorneys, product assemblers, and more. Help is just a phone call away. All you have to do is tell the temp service what you need and it takes care of everything from screening applicants to checking references.

ASSOCIATION SOURCES

Business, trade, and professional associations are another important resource for your business, providing advice, information, and support that can enable you to operate more efficiently. Organized to serve the specific needs of their members, associations can:

▶ Keep you posted on issues affecting your business
▶ Provide education and training programs
▶ Communicate with the media
▶ Lobby government on industry matters
▶ Provide networking opportunities

Whatever type of business you have, you should be able to find associations that represent your industry or area of expertise, whether it's in technology, food service, construction, retailing, finance, health care, or other fields.

One association that promotes the needs of business in general and can be a strong source of ongoing support for entrepreneurs is your local *chamber of commerce*. Chambers of commerce are businesses united together. Serving as the business voice in their communities, they work to create a positive climate for business and to provide entrepreneurs with a forum to exchange ideas and information. In addition to providing local business news and economic data about your community, your chamber of commerce can bring you together with other business leaders through its activities and programs.

Other associations geared toward the needs of business include such organizations as the National Federation of Independent Business, National Association of Women Business Owners, Young Entrepreneurs Association, U.S. Hispanic Chamber of Commerce, and the National Family Business Council.

To locate the trade or professional associations for your particular field or that represent business interests, look in the *Encyclopedia of Associations* in your library's reference section.

ACADEMIC SOURCES

Colleges and universities can also serve a vital support function for your business, offering an array of information and assistance free of charge or at a nominal fee. For example, the schools located in your area should be able to provide you with access to such resources as:

▶ **Library facilities** to use in researching the marketplace and staying current on business issues.
▶ **Classes and seminars** to upgrade your own skills and knowledge and those of employees.

▶ **Consulting advice** provided by faculty members and students in business, engineering, science, and other fields.
▶ **Labor** provided by student interns and part-time workers.

To provide students with real world experience and help faculty members keep their professional skills sharp, many schools strive to maintain an alliance between academia and business. For example, college and university business departments often operate *consulting programs* in which teams of students help local businesses to achieve specific objectives—develop a mailing list, speed up order processing, come up with new products, create training materials, and so on. In addition to this, most *small business development centers* (described earlier in this chapter) are cosponsored by colleges and universities.

As a result of efforts like these, schools throughout the United States have become training centers and information clearinghouses on small business management.

To find out more about the academic resources available to you, contact the business departments and libraries at the colleges and universities in your area.

GETTING YOUR MONEY'S WORTH

It should be reassuring to know the wealth of outside resources available to you when help is needed; and it makes good economic sense to use it. Given the complexity of today's business environment and the competitive pressure to do things faster and better than before, more and more businesses are turning to outsiders for help. Working on an hourly or contractual basis, consultants and other independent contractors can do what needs to be done at a cost that's generally lower than if you hired an employee to do it; but to get your money's worth, you have to know *when* to use outside help and *what* to look for in choosing a consultant or service provider.

When to Use Outside Help

Business situations that would normally benefit from using outside help include:

1. **When you don't have the necessary expertise.** Going outside for help can provide the skills and knowledge you need. Using an export broker for help in entering foreign markets or a public relations firm to generate favorable publicity about your business are both examples of this.

2. **When you have a deadline to meet.** Bringing in outside help can get the work done fast, without having to go through a lengthy process to recruit and train new employees.

3. **When you need an objective viewpoint.** Since an outsider doesn't have a vested interest in the outcome of a decision, he or she is more likely to "tell it like it is." The outsider's distance from your business also provides a different perspective that can be valuable, helping you to see things you may not have noticed.

4. **When you want to build credibility.** Bringing in an outside expert to perform a task or assist in making a decision is a way to show others that you're committed to doing the job right. It can also build trust. For example, hiring a well-known marketing research firm to conduct a study about your products adds credibility to the research data that's obtained.

5. **When you're going through a crisis.** An outside expert, who's skilled in handling the kind of problem you're facing, may be able to turn the situation around. For example, if you're having difficulty maintaining quality levels or need

money to grow, an expert in quality control or financing may help to solve the problem.

6. **When you don't want to do the work.** There may be times when you could do the work yourself or with existing employees, but would rather someone else did it. For example, the work may be unpleasant or increase your liability risk; or it might not be cost-effective for you to do it.

What to Look For

In going outside for help, some of the things you should look for in choosing a consultant or service are:

- ► Ability to do the work
- ► Knowledge of your industry
- ► Reliability
- ► Honesty and integrity
- ► Experience
- ► Human relations skills
- ► Fees that are reasonable

It's important that the person or company you choose is capable of meeting your needs within the specified time frame. The more industry knowledge and experience the individual has, the less explaining you'll have to do about your situation. The human relations skills and temperament of the people you'll be working with should also be taken into consideration. To work well together, you must feel comfortable with them and be able to communicate effectively. You will also need to look closely at the fees you'll be charged to determine if they are competitive and in line with your budget.

Before you make your choice it's essential that you go over the details of what your relationship will be—the work to be

done, how performance is to be measured, start/stop dates,
payment procedures, and so on. To avoid problems later, it's
critical that you have a "meeting of the minds" on what you
need and what's being provided. And, as a final precaution, ask
for references and follow up on them to verify what you've been
told.

IRS TAX PUBLICATIONS

The publications listed below can provide you with additional
information about business taxation. They should be available
at your local IRS office, or you can obtain them by writing to
the Internal Revenue Service, Washington, D.C. 20224.

TITLE	PUBLICATION NO.
Your Rights as a Taxpayer	1
Employer's Tax Guide (Circular E)	15
Your Federal Income Tax	17
Tax Guide for Small Business	334
Fuel Tax Credits and Refunds	378
Travel, Entertainment and Gift Expenses	463
Tax Withholding and Estimated Tax	505
Excise Taxes	510
Taxable and Nontaxable Income	525
Charitable Contributions	526
Miscellaneous Deductions	529
Self-Employment Tax	533
Depreciation	534
Business Expenses	535
Net Operating Losses	536
Accounting Periods and Methods	538
Tax Information on Partnerships	541
Tax Information on Corporations	542
Sales and Other Dispositions of Assets	544
Investment Income and Expenses	550
Basis of Assets	551
Recordkeeping for Individuals	552

TITLE	PUBLICATION NO.
Examinations of Returns, Appeal Rights, and Claims for Refund	556
Retirement Plans for the Self-Employed	560
Taxpayers Starting a Business	583
The Collection Process (Income Tax Accounts)	586A
Business Use of Your Home	587
Tax Information on S Corporations	589
Individual Retirement Accounts (IRAs)	590
The Collection Process (Employment Tax Accounts)	594
Guide to Free Tax Services	910
Tax Information for Direct Sellers	911
Business Use of a Car	917
Employment Taxes and Information Returns	937
How to Begin Depreciating Your Property	946
Filing Requirements for Employee Benefit Plans	1048
Per Diem Rates	1542

SMALL BUSINESS ADMINISTRATION PUBLICATIONS

The publications listed below can provide you with additional information about growing a business. These can be purchased for a nominal fee by writing to the Small Business Administration, Washington, D.C. 20417.

TITLE	PUBLICATION NO.
PRODUCTS/IDEAS/INVENTIONS	
Ideas Into Dollars	PI1
Avoiding Patent, Trademark and Copyright Problems	PI2
Trademarks and Business Goodwill	PI3
FINANCIAL MANAGEMENT	
ABC's of Borrowing	FM1
Profit Costing and Pricing for Manufacturers	FM2
Basic Budgets for Profit Planning	FM3
Understanding Cash Flow	FM4
A Venture Capital Primer for Small Business	FM5
Accounting Services for Small Service Firms	FM6
Analyze Your Records to Reduce Costs	FM7

TITLE	PUBLICATION NO.
Budgeting in a Small Service Firm	FM8
Sound Cash Management and Borrowing	FM9
Record Keeping in a Small Business	FM10
Simple Break-Even Analysis for Small Stores	FM11
A Pricing Checklist for Small Retailers	FM12
Pricing Your Products and Services Profitably	FM13

MANAGEMENT AND PLANNING

Effective Business Communications	MP1
Locating or Relocating Your Business	MP2
Problems in Managing a Family-Owned Business	MP3
Business Plan for Small Manufacturers	MP4
Business Plan for Small Construction Firms	MP5
Planning and Goal Setting for Small Business	MP6
Should You Lease or Buy Equipment?	MP8
Business Plan for Retailers	MP9
Choosing a Retail Location	MP10
Business Plan for Small Service Firms	MP11
Checklist for Going into Business	MP12
How to Get Started with a Small Business Computer	MP14
The Business Plan for Home-Based Business	MP15
How to Buy or Sell a Business	MP16
Purchasing for Owners of Small Plants	MP17
Buying for Retail Stores	MP18
Small Business Decision Making	MP19
Business Continuation Planning	MP20
Developing a Strategic Business Plan	MP21
Inventory Management	MP22
Techniques for Problem Solving	MP23
Techniques for Productivity Improvement	MP24
Selecting the Legal Structure for Your Business	MP25
Evaluating Franchise Opportunities	MP26
Small Business Risk Management Guide	MP28
Quality Child Care Makes Good Business Sense	MP29

MARKETING

Creative Selling: The Competitive Edge	MT1
Marketing for Small Business: An Overview	MT2

TITLE	PUBLICATION NO.
Is the Independent Sales Agent for You?	MT3
Marketing Checklist for Small Retailers	MT4
Researching Your Market	MT8
Selling by Mail Order	MT9
Market Overseas with U.S. Government Help	MT10
Advertising	MT11

CRIME PREVENTION

Curtailing Crime—Inside and Out	CP2
A Small Business Guide to Computer Security	CP3

PERSONNEL MANAGEMENT

Checklist for Developing a Training Program	PM1
Employees: How to Find and Pay Them	PM2
Managing Employee Benefits	PM3

SMALL BUSINESS ADMINISTRATION FIELD OFFICES

Region I
155 Federal St.
9th Fl.
Boston, MA 02110
617-451-2030

Region II
26 Federal Plaza
Rm. 31–08
New York, NY 10278
212-264-7772

Region III
Allendale Square
Ste. 201
475 Allendale Rd.
King of Prussia, PA 19406
215-962-3805

Region IV
1375 Peachtree St., NE
5th Fl.
Atlanta, GA 30367-8102
404-347-2797

Region V
300 S. Riverside Plaza
Ste. 1975
Chicago, IL 60606-6611
312-353-0359

Region VI
8625 King George Dr.
Bldg. C
Dallas, TX 75235-3391
214-767-7643

Region VII
911 Walnut St.
13th Fl.
Kansas City, MO 64106
816-426-2989

Region VIII
999 18th St.
Ste. 701, N. Tower
Denver, CO 80202
303-294-7001

Region IX
71 Stevenson St.
San Francisco, CA 94105-2939
415-744-6402

Region X
2615 Fourth Ave.
Rm. 440
Seattle, WA 98121
206-442-5676

SMALL BUSINESS DEVELOPMENT CENTERS (SBDCs)

ALABAMA	University of Alabama at Birmingham 1717 11th Ave. South, Ste. 419 Birmingham, AL 35294	(205) 934-7260
ALASKA	University of Alaska, Anchorage 430 W. 7th Ave., Ste. 110 Anchorage, AK 99501	(907) 274-7232
ARIZONA	Arizona SBDC Network 9215 N. Canyon Hwy. Phoenix, AZ 85021	(602) 943-2311
ARKANSAS	University of Arkansas 100 South Main St., Ste. 401 Little Rock, AR 72201	(501) 324-9043
CALIFORNIA	Department of Commerce Small Business Development Center 801 K St., Ste. 1700 Sacramento, CA 95814	(916) 324-5068

COLORADO	Small Business Development Center Office of Business Development 1625 Broadway, Ste. 1710 Denver, CO 80202	(303) 892-3809
CONNECTICUT	University of Connecticut 368 Fairfield Rd., SBA U-41, Rm. 422 Storrs, CT 06269	(203) 486-4135
DELAWARE	University of Delaware Purnell Hall, Ste. 005 Newark, NJ 19716	(302) 831-2747
DISTRICT OF COLUMBIA	Howard University Small Business Development Center 2600 Sixth St., Room 128 Washington, D.C. 20059	(202) 806-1550
FLORIDA	University of West Florida Florida SBDC Network Bldg. 76, Rm. 231 Pensacola, FL 32514	(904) 474-3016
GEORGIA	University of Georgia 1180 E. Broad St. Athens, GA 30602	(404) 542-5760
HAWAII	Hawaii SBDC Network University of Hawaii at Hilo 523 W. Lanikaula St. Hilo, HI 96720	(808) 933-3515
IDAHO	Boise State University College of Business 1910 University Dr. Boise, ID 83725	(208) 835-1640
ILLINOIS	Department of Commerce & Community Affairs 620 East Adams St. Springfield, IL 62701	(217) 524-5856

INDIANA	Indiana SBDC One North Capital, Ste. 420 Indianapolis, IN 46204	(317) 264-6871
IOWA	Iowa SBDC Iowa State University Chamberlain Bldg., 137 Lynn Ave. Ames, IA 50010	(515) 292-6351
KANSAS	Wichita State University 1845 Fairmont, 21 Clinton Hall Wichita, KS 67208	(316) 689-3193
KENTUCKY	University of Kentucky 225 Business and Economics Bldg. Lexington, KY 40506	(606) 257-7668
LOUISIANA	Northeast Louisiana University College of Business University Dr. Monroe, LA 71209	(318) 342-5506
MAINE	University of Southern Maine 96 Falmouth St. Portland, ME 04103	(207) 780-4420
MARYLAND	Maryland SBDC Network State Administrative Office Dept. of Econ. & Employment Devel. 217 East Redwood St., 10th Fl. Baltimore, MD 21202	(410) 333-6996
MASSACHUSETTS	University of Massachusetts 205 School of Management Amherst, MA 01003	(413) 545-6301

MICHIGAN	Wayne State University 2727 Second Ave. Detroit, MI 48201	(313) 577-4848
MINNESOTA	Dept. of Trade and Economic Devel. 900 American Center Bldg. 150 East Kellogg Blvd. St. Paul, MN 55101	(612) 297-5770
MISSISSIPPI	Small Business Development Ctr. Old Chemistry Bldg., Ste. 216 University, MS 38677	(601) 232-5001
MISSOURI	MO SBDC University of Missouri 300 University Pl. Columbia, MO 65211	(314) 882-0344
MONTANA	Helena SBDC Montana Department of Commerce 1424 Ninth Ave. Helena, MT 59620	(406) 444-4780
NEBRASKA	University of Nebraska at Omaha College of Business Administration Bldg. 60th & Dodge, Rm. 407 Omaha, NE 68182	(402) 554-2521
NEVADA	University of Nevada, Reno College of Bus. Admin., Rm. 411 Reno, NV 89557	(702) 784-1717
NEW HAMPSHIRE	University of New Hampshire 108 McConnell Hall Durham, NH 03824	(603) 862-2200

NEW JERSEY	Small Business Development Center Rutgers University 180 University Ave. 3rd Fl., Ackerson Hall Newark, NJ 07102	(201) 648-5950
NEW MEXICO	NMSBDC Lead Center Santa Fe Community College P.O. Box 4187 Santa Fe, NM 87502	(505) 438-1362
NEW YORK	State University of New York SUNY Central Administration S-523 Albany, NY 12246	(518) 443-5398
NORTH CAROLINA	University of North Carolina 4509 Creedmoor Rd., Ste. 201 Raleigh, NC 27612	(919) 733-4643
NORTH DAKOTA	University of North Dakota 118 Gamble Hall, UND Grand Forks, ND 58202	(701) 777-3700
OHIO	Small Business Development Center 77 South High St. Columbus, OH 43226	(614) 466-2711
OKLAHOMA	Southeastern Oklahoma State University Station A Box 2584 Durant, OK 74701	(405) 924-0277
OREGON	Lane Community College 99 W. 10th Ave., Ste. 216 Eugene, OR 97401	(503) 726-2250

PENNSYLVANIA	University of Pennsylvania The Wharton School 444 Vance Hall Philadelphia, PA 19104	(215) 898-1219
PUERTO RICO	University of Puerto Rico Mayaguez Campus, Box 5253 Mayaguez, PR 00681	(809) 834-3590
RHODE ISLAND	Bryant College SBDC 1150 Douglas Pike Smithfield, RI 02917	(401) 232-6111
SOUTH CAROLINA	University of South Carolina College of Business Administration Columbia, SC 29208	(803) 777-4907
SOUTH DAKOTA	University of South Dakota Business Research Bureau 414 E. Clark St. Vermillion, SD 57069	(605) 677-5272
TENNESSEE	Memphis State University Bldg. 1, South Campus Memphis, TN 38152	(901) 678-2500
TEXAS	Dallas SBDC Bill J. Priest Institute for Economic Development 1402 Corinth St. Dallas, TX 75215	(214) 565-5833
UTAH	University of Utah 102 West 500 South, Ste. 315 Salt Lake City, UT 84101	(801) 581-7905
VERMONT	Vermont SBDC 1 Blair Park, Ste. 13 Williston, VT 05495	(802) 878-0181

VIRGINIA	Virginia SBDC Department of Economic Development P.O. Box 798, 1021 East Cary St. Richmond, VA 23219	(804) 371-8258
VIRGIN ISLANDS	University of the Virgin Islands P.O. Box 1087 St. Thomas, VI 00804	(809) 776-3206
WASHINGTON	Washington State University 245 Todd Hall Pullman, WA 99164	(509) 335-1576
WEST VIRGINIA	West Virginia SBDC Governor's Office of Community & Industrial Development 1115 Virginia St. Charleston, WV 25301	(304) 348-2960
WISCONSIN	University of Wisconsin 432 North Lake St., Rm. 423 Madison, WI 53706	(608) 263-7794
WYOMING	WSBDC/State Network Office 111 W. 2nd St., Ste. 416 Casper, WY 82601	(307) 235-4825

16

THE
NEXT
STEP

Sooner or later, everyone who grows a business reaches the point when they must look ahead to the future and determine what new directions they want their businesses to go or new roles they want to play in shaping them.

At that point, given what you've accomplished, you must decide what you want to do next. Do you want to be more or less involved in your business? To give family members greater roles? Take in partners? Merge with another business? Sell off? Reenter the corporate world? Retire? Start another business to grow?

ASSESSING YOUR ROLE

Perhaps the most critical decision you must make as an entrepreneur is what your role in the business is going to be. Do you want to maintain your current level of involvement? Cut back? Get even more involved? This decision is especially important because it not only affects your future lifestyle and financial security, but those of the people around you.

Although some entrepreneurs find this decision easier to make than others, it's not an easy decision by any means. That's because each entrepreneur and each situation is different.

Obvious factors, such as age, health, and personal finances, must be considered, but others come into play, too. Have you met your goals? Is the business personally satisfying and challenging? Are there other opportunities you want to pursue? Do family members have the willingness and capability to run the business? How easy would it be to sell it? How do you want to spend your time?

The same effort and planning that went into growing your business, must now go into assessing your role in it and determining whether to continue on your present path or choose a new one. There are many choices to be made and the best way to make the right ones is by preparing for them.

KEEPING IT IN THE FAMILY

One of the goals for many entrepreneurs is to grow a business that they can eventually turn over to their children or other family members to run, keeping it in the family from one generation to the next. As commonly held a goal as this is, it can be one of the hardest to reach unless you take the time to develop a *succession plan* and to groom your successor to take over the business. A simple task, you might think, and it *should* be. But one has only to look at the numerous book and movie plots based on family business struggles or pick up a newspaper, to know that it can be more difficult than it appears.

The time to begin planning for your succession is long before the event will take place. Children and others who are being considered as future leaders of the business need to be trained to assume greater responsibilities and given time to grow into the roles they will be performing. Along with this, their own needs and preferences, talents and abilities must be considered. All too often, children are forced into joining a family-owned business or pushed into positions that they are unsuited for without giving any thought to what *they* want to do. A recipe for disappointment and dissatisfaction on *both* sides of the generation gap, this can not only lead to the break-up of the business, but also of the family.

By combining forethought and sensitivity, you can avoid the problems that often arise when it's time to turn over the helm to the next generation of entrepreneurs. Some of the things you can do to make the transition go more smoothly include

1. **Recognizing the inevitable.** Nothing keeps going forever—with the possible exception of the Energizer Rabbit. If you want your business to outlast you, you must take action to have a successor in place when you're ready to step down.

2. **Getting your children involved from the start.** Talking about the business and giving your children opportunities to work in it while they're growing up is a good way to give them a feel for it and to find out where their interests lie. Starting at the bottom and learning about each aspect of the business not only builds skills and character, but can help your children to determine how (and *if*) they want to participate in running the business.

3. **Assessing your children objectively.** Rather than automatically turning over the business to one child or another—the eldest, for instance—it's important to determine which one is the most capable of handling the responsibilities. Putting your emotions aside, this entails looking at each child's qualifications and temperament and, as objectively as possible, assessing who would make the best leader. In some instances, it means accepting the fact that your children may *not* be the

ones most suited to succeed you; in which case you need to identify someone else in your business or look outside for a candidate.

4. **Developing a succession plan.** Telling your children that "one day this will all be yours" isn't much of a plan. A detailed plan needs to be worked out showing *when* and *how* the transition is to take place, and the amount of authority you will continue to have. For example, are you going to hold another position in the business? serve on the board of directors? act as an outside consultant?

5. **Getting professional help.** To make sure that your succession plan works as it's intended, you should get help in preparing it. An accountant and an attorney can help you to go over the financial and legal aspects of it. And, for good measure, you might consider using the services of a family business consultant to help work out the personal side of it. If your business is a corporation, the board of directors should also be actively involved in this process.

In addition, you should encourage your children to get as much education and outside work experience as they can. Knowing your business inside out is important, but your children also need to know how other businesses operate and to have the experience of doing something "on their own," rather than just stepping into your shoes.

JOINING FORCES

As your business grows, another option that you may want to consider is joining forces with someone else—taking in partners or merging with another business. This can be especially advantageous if you're trying to get a bigger share of the market but lack the capital or other resources (personnel, technology, distribution network, and so on) to carry out the necessary activities to do it. By joining forces, rather than going it alone, you can obtain the resources you need to accomplish your objectives. The only catch, of course, is making sure you choose the right people or business to team up with as partners.

Taking in Partners

If you're thinking about letting someone from outside your business buy into it or about elevating an employee to the level of partner, then you want to consider the new relationship carefully. What could that person contribute to the business? What would he or she get in return? How would you work together? Are you willing to share ownership and decision-making authority? Would it put you in a better position to carry out your plans?

Since it's a lot easier to enter into a partnership than it is to get out of one, this decision shouldn't be rushed. The warning, "Act in haste, repent at leisure," applies all too well here.

Merging with Another Business

The same factors that need to be considered in taking in a partner also need to be considered here, but on a larger scale. Now, rather than determining how your methods and objectives mesh with another's, you must determine how your entire business organization meshes with another business organization. In addition to looking at how the two businesses operate—what they do and what they want to accomplish—you must look at their *corporate cultures* as well, to assess their compatibility.

As with a marriage, finding someone you can *live* with after the courtship and honeymoon are over is the most important factor. Often a potential merger partner can look good on paper, with a solid balance sheet and a good revenue stream, but the business can be impossible to work with—a point that's sometimes not known until *after* the merger.

In choosing a merger partner, among the things to consider are its:

- Products or services
- Target markets
- Location/facilities
- Marketing methods
- Size
- Experience and stability
- Financial situation
- Image and reputation
- Growth potential
- Objectives
- Corporate culture

Ideally you should be able to complement each other, one of you providing added strength in the areas where the other is the weakest. For example, one company may have the production capability, but not the distribution network, or one may have facilities in the West but not in the East. If the other business can provide what's missing, so much the better.

No matter how good everything looks, though, if you have problems with the corporate culture, stop and think. Then think *again*.

In looking at another business's corporate culture and evaluating whether or not it is compatible with yours, some of the areas to focus on are

How authority is distributed. Is the organization centralized or decentralized? Are decisions made from the top-down or the bottom-up? Unilaterally or by consensus?

The degree of formality that exists. Do people interact on a first-name basis? Is there an open- or closed-door environment? Is information conveyed orally or in writing? Face-to-face or through memos? Are employees more likely to wear suits or jeans to work? Is the atmosphere warm or cold? Serious or playful?

The policies and procedures that are followed. How and when are meetings held? What are the procedures or guidelines for carrying out activities—hiring personnel, handling paperwork, traveling on business, reporting expenses, and so on?

The behaviors that are valued. Is the emphasis more on individual accomplishment or on being part of a team? Competition or cooperation? Creative or analytic skills? Following the rules or breaking them? A free-wheeling approach or conservative? Putting the business first or family? Getting along or getting ahead? Blending in or standing out?

The attitude toward risks. Is the business more inclined to take risks or avoid them? Go slow or go for broke? Be a leader or a follower?

Much of it comes down to matters of style and personality, the beliefs that are held and how things are done. Although they might be seen only as minor details or something to be worked out later, if they're incompatible they can make it impossible for the two businesses to function. The more similar the two cultures are, the stronger the corporate union will be.

SELLING THE BUSINESS

If you're not planning on keeping the business in the family and you're ready to go on to something else, then it's time to give serious thought to selling your business. Assessing the pros and cons, the money you stand to gain, the timing, and how this fits in with your overall objectives, you need to look long and hard at this option. Countless decisions went into growing your business, but it takes only *one* to sell it. You want to make certain it's the right one.

The Reasons to Sell

There are many reasons for selling a business. For example:

▶ You've accomplished your objectives and are looking for new challenges unrelated to the business.
▶ You've built up considerable equity in the business and want to cash out.
▶ You've received an offer you can't refuse.
▶ You want to retire.
▶ You want to move to another city.
▶ You want to return to the corporate world.
▶ You've "burned out" on the business and don't want to run it anymore.
▶ You have health or family problems.

Whatever the reason may be, you need to examine it thoroughly and make sure that it is a valid one for selling the business and, in so doing, that you would achieve the desired outcome. If the business is just starting to peak, for instance, by selling now, would you be bailing out too early and missing out on the chance to receive a higher price for it? Or, if you want new challenges, could the business go in those new directions, too? As for entrepreneur burn-out or the desire to retire, could these be met simply by delegating more authority or by reorganizing the business so that your role in it is different?

After giving it more thought, if your reasons for wanting to sell hold up and you are convinced that this is the best way to go, your next step is to put together a marketing strategy for selling the business.

Marketing the Business

Like selling a house, there's more to selling a business than putting up a "For Sale" sign and waiting for the offers to come in. You have to (1) get it ready to go on the market, (2) show it to its best advantage—to the *right* prospects, and (3) negotiate the sale.

1. Getting Ready to Sell

To get the business ready to go on the market you should start by

▶ **Preparing a business plan** or updating your existing one to adequately reflect your current circumstances and highlight the business's accomplishments, goals, and objectives.
▶ **Putting your finances in order** and having your statements for the past three to five years audited by a certified public accountant.
▶ **Dealing with legal matters,** ensuring that employment contracts, supplier and lease agreements, and so on can be readily transferred to the buyer and that any pending litigation is resolved.
▶ **Informing employees of your decision to sell** and taking action to minimize any anxiety they may feel about it and to enlist their support in the selling process.
▶ **Finding a competent business broker or mergers and acquisitions specialist** to assist you in targeting potential buyers and handling the sales negotiations.

2. Showcasing the Business

To make your business look its best and gain the interest of potential buyers, it helps to prepare a *sales document* that specifically highlights the key benefits associated with purchasing the business. Emphasizing the business's strengths, the sales document is to give investors an inside look at the business and a feel for what it does and is capable of doing in the future. Going beyond the business plan, which functions like a blueprint, it is meant to function like an artist's rendering, depicting the actual business itself. In this regard, particular attention should be given to such factors as proprietary products or processes that belong to the business alone, customer loyalty, market strength, management capabilities, modern facilities, and so on.

Once the sales document is completed and you and your adviser have identified likely prospects, you can begin to contact the ones you think will be the most interested in buying the business. Among the potential buyers to keep in mind here are your *competitors, suppliers, customers,* and *employees.* Others include *businesses in related fields* and *businesses with large cash reserves,* as well as *prospective entrepreneurs* who would rather buy a business than start one.

During the marketing phase, it's important to showcase the business to a large enough number of potential buyers to ensure that you get the best price for it. At the same time, though, you have to be careful not to harm the business by neglecting its day-to-day operations or jeopardizing the confidentiality of critical information. In marketing the business to competitors, for instance, you want to provide them with enough information to make a purchase decision, but not enough to use against you in a competitive situation.

3. Negotiating the Sale

Once you've narrowed the field of prospective buyers to the most serious and qualified ones, you're ready to consider their offers and come to an agreement with the buyer whose offer provides the best combination of purchase price and payment terms.

Equally important as the money that is paid for the business is the *form* and *timing* of the payments you receive. For example, will the payment be made in one lump sum of cash up front, in installments, or in shares of stock in the acquiring company?

Getting the money *up front* gives you the advantage of knowing that the money is yours and being able to put it to immediate use; but the tax consequences can severely lower your net proceeds from the sale.

The *installment* method lets you defer your tax obligation until the payments are received, spreading it out over a number of years; but this limits your ability to utilize the funds and, if something goes wrong with the business down the road, you could have difficulty collecting the money that is owed to you.

By accepting the payment in *shares of stock* (swapping your stock for theirs), there's no tax liability until you actually sell the stock; and if the stock goes up, you could end up getting even more for your business. On the other hand, there are likely to be limitations on when you can sell the stock, and if it goes down, you stand to lose money.

To negotiate the best terms, you and your adviser will have to balance the need for liquidity against the need to lower your taxes. You'll also have to look at the level of risk that you're willing to accept and your short- and long-term objectives. It's also important to remember that, in addition to the financial aspects of the sale, there are the *psychological* aspects to consider. You need to be aware of your feelings and emotions about the sale and work to reach an agreement that you feel comfortable with; one that not only enhances your net worth, but your *self* worth.

FINDING NEW CHALLENGES

Perhaps you'd like to take what you've learned as an entrepreneur growing your business and put it to use back in the corporate world working for someone else. Or maybe you'd like to become an oxymoron, enjoying an "active retirement," spending more time with your family and friends. Or it just might be that you'd like to do it all over again and grow your *next* business.

Whatever you decide, the choice is yours, just as it was in the beginning. Whether you continue as an entrepreneur or go on to something else, the important thing is to keep looking for new challenges and ways to get satisfaction out of life.

In answering the question, "What's next?" you need to take stock of where you are and where you want to go; then begin the journey, keeping in mind as you go the words of Robert Frost:

The woods are lovely, dark and deep.
But I have promises to keep,
And miles to go before I sleep,
And miles to go before I sleep.

There is still much to be done. You can continue to nurture the business that you've grown, take time to harvest the fruits of your labor, or plant another seed . . . and begin the cycle again.

INDEX